KB.
1986.

One Man's Advent

Antony Bridge was born in 1914. He won a
scholarship to the Royal Academy School
of Art in 1932 and earned his living as an
artist until joining the army in 1939. After
the war he resumed his career as a painter
but in the early 1950s decided to enter the
Church and was ordained in 1955. From
1958 to 1968 he was Vicar of Christ
Church, Lancaster Gate. He has been
Dean of Guildford since 1968.

He is the author of *Theodora*, a life of
the Byzantine Empress; *Suleiman the
Magnificent*; and *The Crusades*. He is a
regular lecturer on cruises in the Mediterranean and broadcasts frequently on
radio and television.

ANTONY BRIDGE

One Man's Advent

Collins
FOUNT PAPERBACKS

First published in Great Britain
by Granada Publishing, London in 1985
Third impression (under the new name
of Grafton Books) January 1986
Published by Fount Paperbacks, London 1986

Made and printed in Great Britain by
William Collins Sons & Co. Ltd, Glasgow

Extracts from T. S. Eliot reprinted by
permission of Faber and Faber Ltd from
Collected Poems 1909–1962 by T. S. Eliot

'Vers de Société' reprinted by
permission of Faber and Faber Ltd from
High Windows by Philip Larkin

Extract from 'In Westminster Abbey' reprinted by
permission of John Murray (Publishers) Ltd from
Collected Poems by John Betjeman

Contents

'It is time for us to draw the lessons from twentieth-century post-mechanistic science, and to get out of the straitjacket which nineteenth-century materialism imposed on our philosophical outlook. Paradoxically, had that outlook kept abreast with modern science itself, instead of lagging a century behind it, we should have been liberated from that straitjacket long ago.'

Arthur Koestler,
The Roots of Coincidence

Preface

One of the difficulties of writing a book about belief and unbelief is that there is a sense in which there is no such thing as belief but only someone who believes something or other, or does not do so. All statements about belief in the abstract diminish the reality of believing or disbelieving, reducing it, in fact, to a set of propositions about belief; and that is a very different and often a very dangerous thing. All Churches have drawn up such propositional tables, pleading practical necessity and arguing that their beliefs have to be precisely defined if anyone is to know what they are; but while in a sense this is true, again and again the results have been disastrous, Christians proving their orthodoxy by signing on the dotted line to one or other set of doctrinal formulations, Orthodox or Monophysite, Protestant or Catholic, and then hurrying away to burn those who disagree with them. Of course, Christians are not the only people who have indulged in this kind of behaviour; the men of Stalin's Russia with their persecution of deviationists and the bloodthirsty mullahs of the Ayatollah's Iran have provided recent examples of the same lethal behaviour.

Yet another reason for remembering that belief is not an abstraction and cannot be separated from the person who believes is the obvious fact that what a man believes is at least partly – and often almost entirely – a product of his time, place and social setting; for example, if I had been born a Chinese peasant, the chances of me ending my life as a priest in the Church of England would not have constituted much of a threat to members of the Chinese bookmaking profession. So any statement about someone who believes something or other, be it that which a Christian, a Buddhist, a humanist or a Communist believes, must start with an account, however minimal, of the believer himself and of the people and the experiences which have helped to make him what he is and have therefore contributed to the formation of his belief or unbelief. So the first part of this book will have to be a brief account of myself and of some of the experiences which seem to me in retrospect to have been both germinal and formative; and indeed the link which binds the book together, for better or for worse, must inevitably be a personal one.

However, the personal factor in belief is by no means the end of the matter. If it were, there would be no means of evaluating the respective beliefs of – say – Hitler, Karl Marx and Christ. Therefore at some point in what follows I shall try to look at the problem of credibility and how it may be established, and this will also involve a look at the contemporary fragmentation of man and the alienation of his intellect from the other departments of his being: the alienation perhaps of the right hemisphere of his brain from the left, and the similar and perhaps partly consequent alienation of man from his natural environment; for one of my firmest convictions is that when the analytical intellect is isolated from other modes of apprehension – artistic, intuitive, emotional and passive – we tend to stop living our lives, assuming instead the role of spectators. In an essay on pornography, D. H. Lawrence said that 'sex in the head kills sex in the bed' or words to that effect, and his aphorism can be extended to cover the intellectualizing of other departments of human experience. Goethe knew this. 'Grey is all theory, green is life's growing tree,' he said, and Coleridge said much the same thing when he insisted that 'Our meddling intellect misshapes the beauteous forms of things. We murder to dissect.' But this does not mean that I am hostile to the analytical intellect or that I agree with Luther who dubbed reason 'that whore'. On the contrary, I believe what I believe with my intellect, not despite it. But perhaps the heart of my conviction is that the experience of being, art, faith and reason are inseparable parts of the human vision of reality; for as we sit in the solitary chambers of our heads, we have those four windows — being, art, faith and reason — through which that-which-is may reveal itself to us, and only when we use all of them are we likely to get a vision of reality approximating to the whole truth.

To the child in the snow

I

Genetics and Environment

My father was a naval officer with a remarkably good brain and few morals; he passed examinations almost in his sleep, outdoing all his competitors in the process, but he had little or no respect for the conventional bourgeois moral standards of the day. At the age of fourteen or thereabouts, after a number of years at the naval school at Dartmouth, he was despatched to Hong Kong to join the Royal Navy there as a midshipman. He travelled by passenger ship by way of the Suez Canal and India, and although it was customary at the time for boys of his age to begin their naval careers while still so young, it was probably less customary for them to be introduced to some of the other adult delights which came my father's way on the voyage; for during its course he was seduced by a young married woman who was travelling to India to join her husband there, and he spent much of his time at sea in bed with her. He seems to have enjoyed this way of passing the time so much that he became addicted to it, and thereafter he seduced whom he could, when he could and as he could, which was frequently, for he was highly attractive to women: at least, that was my mother's version of events, and I have no reason to doubt that it was substantially true. Personally, I never knew him, and I am not even sure that the one memory I have of him is a genuine memory or the result of being told of the incident later; whichever it may be, it goes back into my earliest childhood. He was standing in front of a mirror in the bathroom shaving and with nothing on, when I toddled in. I think it must be a genuine memory, for I recall coming no higher than his knees. I began to back out again, whereupon he laughed, his face still covered in a white lather of soap, and said, 'Come in! Come in! If you see anything you haven't got yourself, you may hang your hat on it.'

As to my mother, who was born in high Victorian days in 1885, she was ravishingly beautiful in a somewhat patrician way and magnificently irresponsible. Her childhood had not been a happy one; as a result of her birth, my grandmother had had puerperal fever, and thereafter she had never liked my mother while doting on two younger children. Eventually my mother was sent to a large boarding school for girls near the South Coast, from which she promptly absconded, returning home and refusing to go back there in any circumstances: an escapade which did not endear her to her parents or make them any the less strict in their treatment of her. But at the age of about eighteen she began to come into her own and enjoy life; for as soon as she was allowed to appear in public on social occasions she became the centre of attraction for eager young Edwardian suitors who buzzed round her like amorous bees round a nectar-laden blossom. One of them, in something like a caricature of the social *mores* of the time, was a Belgian Count, who tried to besiege her bedroom by way of a ladder, only to be pushed down into the garden by an irate Scottish nurse named Maggie, who was devoted to my mother and determined to defend her virtue against all comers. I do not know how many times she became secretly and unofficially engaged, but I believe it was not a rare event, and she was engaged to someone else when she married my father in 1909. As a woman, she had many faults and shortcomings, some of which were due to her volatile temperament and some to her upbringing, background and the society of her time, but as a mother she was unfailingly loving to me, and I cannot remember ever having a serious row with her; indeed, I am not sure that I ever had a row of any kind with her: disagreements galore and momentary flashes of anger, yes, but anything worth calling a row, virtually never. She could be infuriating, but perhaps because I inherited many of her characteristics and could therefore understand both them and her, I seldom found her so. Retrospectively, I am sure that much of her more aggressive behaviour was bluster: the blustering rebellion of the small child inside her, who had never forgotten the rejections and restrictions of her childhood.

In view of many things, however, it is not surprising that my parents' marriage lasted barely seven years. My father's taste for adultery was greatly facilitated by the outbreak of war in 1914, and his understandable and in some ways rather endearing habit of confessing to my mother that he had yet again succumbed to an adulterous temptation, while begging her to forgive him, did not help the marriage; for when she did indeed forgive him, he was able to go happily to sleep, while she lay awake in misery and heartache. Moreover, his disregard for the moral conventions of the day embraced those governing the rights of private property, and this, too, deeply distressed her; for when and if my father thought that someone could afford to go without something, which he himself wanted to have, as long as the object of his desire was something which he regarded as of no great importance, he had no hesitation in taking it. My mother, with a simple and rather black-and-white moral outlook, was appalled on one occasion when, after a fashionable dance which they had attended together,

my father took someone's gold-headed cane on the
grounds that anyone who could afford to buy such a
thing in the first place could well afford to buy another.
It was a kind of practical communism with which she
could not come to terms and, taken together with many
other things, it led them to the divorce courts. It did not
do so, however, before they had had three children, of
whom I was the second, conceived I believe in a Swed-
ish hotel in the closing days of 1913 before the old world
fell apart in war and mud. It was typical of my mother's
unconventional candour that, one day after we had both
had a couple of drinks before luncheon, she should have
told me where I had been conceived.

Of my earliest childhood up to the age of about seven,
a few unrelated incidents stand out in my memory as
though lit up by flashes of summer lightning in the
otherwise undifferentiated darkness of that forgotten
time: my brother's birth, when I was two and a half, and
the remembrance of stepping down a step in a doorway
on to a rose-coloured carpet in a white room to be told
that he had been born; picking a dark purple and white
pansy for a man in a white suit who was sitting on a
white-painted garden bench with my mother, also
dressed in white, in front, I believe, of a white house;
being told by my grandfather's cook, Alice, a rather
gaunt old woman with a light moustache, of someone
who had caught a chill and had died vomiting excre-
ment: an old wives' tale, I now recognize, to frighten me
into being careful not to catch a chill, but horrifyingly
real and memorable at the time; later being taken to see
old Alice in the local hospital, where she was dying of
cancer and looking like a bag of bones in a fine, polished,
waxy skin, her eyes alone large, dark, alive and
unhappy; watching four men kill a pig, held down on its
back by its legs and squealing, and the bubbling noise as

one of the men cut its throat with a knife. For some reason, the purple pansy and the man and my mother in white made the biggest impression on me, as though that moment and its white and purple luminescence held a special significance, nearly but not quite breaking through the surface of triviality and revealing its secret to me. It was the first of a number of similar experiences which have punctuated my life, and of which for many years I took little notice while still remembering them. In *Janus* (1978) Arthur Koestler compared such moments of increased awareness to the experience of falling through a stage trap-door from the trivial plane of existence, upon which we spend most of our time, on to a plane which he called the tragic or absolute plane; 'then all at once our daily routines appear as shallow, trifling vanities; but once safely back on the trivial plane, we dismiss the experiences of the other as phantasms of overstrung nerves.' But are they? It is a question to which I shall return.

As John Donne observed, 'No man is an island, entire of itself', and my family and social environment had already begun to press me into shape and form me, but it was during my school days that the continent of mankind began to increase the pressure, and the forces exerted were those of the Western European world as it was immediately following the First World War, when the old Europe, born somewhere around AD 1500 of the dying medieval world, was in its turn dying; for as the American philosopher William C. Barrett remarked in his book, *Irrational Man*, (1977):

The First World War was the beginning of the end of the bourgeois civilization of Europe ... It would be superficial to take the outbreak of that war, as Marxists do, as signifying merely the bankruptcy of capitalism, its inability to function without crisis and bloodshed. August 1914 was a much more total *human* débâcle than that ... It revealed that the apparent stability, security and material progress of society had rested, like everything human, upon the void. European man came face to face with himself as a stranger. When he ceased to be contained and sheltered within a stable social and political environment, he saw that his rational and enlightened philosophy could no longer console him with the assurance that it satisfactorily answered the question, What is man?

The First World War may have revealed this to some people at the time, though I rather doubt that it did so to many, and it certainly did not do so to me or, as far as I can judge the matter in retrospect, to my teachers; although I agree that that is what the war of 1914–18 should have revealed to those with eyes to read the signs of the times correctly. Perhaps people chose to be blind in the face of so dark and frightening a prospect. Whether this was the case or not, my teachers were at pains to convince me and the other little boys in their charge that the old world had not passed away; on the contrary, it had survived with its attitudes and its self-understanding unchanged and undarkened by even the smallest doubt about its own infinite superiority to all other worlds past or present. In effect, this meant that the two dominant and semi-contradictory ideologies (for want of a better word), which had informed the pre-war western world, were both still valid and true. The first and most popular was the radically optimistic humanism of the nineteenth century, which had underpinned the works of such men as Karl Marx, Friedrich Engels and Thomas Huxley: an optimism which still lay behind the ideas of H. G. Wells and even Bertrand Russell. According to this school of thought, the great enemies of humanity were poverty and ignorance, both of which had for centuries prevented us from controlling our own destiny. Get rid of poverty by creating new wealth by means of newly discovered industrial techniques, and banish ignorance by dispelling the darkness artificially created by the religious obscurantism of the past, flooding the world with the beneficent light of universal education, and the millennium would be round the corner. The other was a curious kind of more or less conventional and vestigial Christianity, which was normally kept in a separate compartment of the believer's mind from that in which instructions governing the conduct of his daily life were stored: instructions mostly dictated by the humanism of the day; the religious compartment was opened on Sundays, occasionally for prayer, and for such events as marriages and deaths in the family. Its contents were not particularly Christian but rather drearily Stoic with much emphasis upon self-discipline, self-reliance, courage and self-advancement. The aim of life was success, and achieving it involved the acceptance of competition, hardship, and the adoption of a curious double standard of behaviour; on the one hand, one was encouraged to be modest, kind, courteous, socially conformist, and either uninterested in sexual matters or, if that was not always possible, in rigid control of one's erotic urges and determined to simulate indifference to them; while, on the other hand, in academic affairs, games and eventually in business and politics, one had to be self-seeking, ruthless, and single-minded in doing everyone else down in the struggle to excel and succeed. You were allowed to be magnanimous to the vanquished; indeed, it was expected of you; but the overriding priority was first to vanquish your opponents. Meanwhile, if you erred by allowing this aggressive standard of behaviour to invade your personal relationships, you were condemned as socially boorish and a cad, while if you were foolish enough to attempt to be 'Christian' in the competitive world of exams, sport and careers, you were written off as spineless and impractical, a dreamer, a fool and a wet. Of course, there were some people who did not conform to these social conventions, but on the whole most people did so to a greater or lesser extent.

Religion hardly brushed off on me at school. As a child, I believed in God in a vague and superstitious way, but this was a legacy of home rather than school. At my first school near Brighton, to which I was sent at the age of eight, we were marched to church on Sundays in crocodile, two by regimented two, there to attend services which, as I remember them, were unsurpassably drab. The church itself was a large, grey, undistinguished, late Victorian, seaside Gothic edifice, and what went on in it was equally undistinguished and colourless, as indeed was what went on later in the chapel of my next school at Marlborough, where I was summoned by the same bells as had plagued the life out of John Betjeman a year or two earlier. In these places of ecclesiastical assembly – I hesitate to call them 'places of worship', for worship did not seem to me to play much part in either of these gentlemanly shrines dedicated to moral uplift and social conformity – the services were taken by infinitely colourless, short-back-and-sides clergymen in infinitely colourless black and white clothes, who, like ham actors in provincial theatres, assumed over-solemn voices in church, and then shed them with their clothing after the services, reverting to normal, smelling of pipe tobacco and tweed, and speaking with whatever social or regional accent they happened to have acquired from the accident of their birth. The performance in church was a social rite, an act through which one passed in portentous or in simulated solemnity, which I did not understand, but which I felt to be in some obscure way important and in the true sense sacred: that is to say, set apart from ordinary life. Everything underlined this separation of church and life: the way in which the officiating clergy put on different clothes and a different voice was symbolic of the deeper truth of this separation, and although I did not think this through consciously at the time (and I am sure that the clergy themselves did not do so either), it communicated itself plainly enough, so that I and all the other small boys treated the two realms of religion and life as distinct from each other.

None of this meant, however, that the ordinary, everyday world was a one-dimensional place, free of mystery or fear; on the contrary, throughout my childhood it remained a frightening place of shadows, in which certain places, objects and actions had to be avoided. There was a particularly lethal picture at the top of my grandfather's stairs; it was a black and white print of a painting depicting Tennyson's Lady of Shalott at the terrible moment when she had brought the curse, which she had always dreaded, down upon her luckless head.

> She left the web, she left the loom,
> She made three paces thro' the room,
> She saw the water-lily bloom,
> She saw the helmet and the plume,
>   She look'd down to Camelot.
> Out flew the web, and floated wide;
> The mirror crack'd from side to side;
> 'The curse is come upon me,' cried
>   The Lady of Shalott.

And there she was, staring out from the picture with terrifying great dark eyes straight at me as I ran past her,

and I could never run fast enough. Another hazard of
that time was the nasty possibility that I might grow to
be like the person who had happened to sit in the same
bus or train seat as that which I subsequently occupied,
the warmth of whom I could feel permeating me
through my bottom and possibly doing terrible things to
me in the process; and so I could go on. But these
childish fears and fantasies disappeared as I grew into
my teens, as too did what little religious belief I had
managed to acquire in my earliest years. What went on
in church and school chapel still remained separate from
everyday life, but it lost its sacredness, remaining
strictly separate only in the sense that what was said in
ecclesiastical buildings and what was done outside them
was – or anyway seemed to me to be – a different thing
altogether. Schoolmasters spoke of love and forgiveness
in chapel and beat you in school; you were encouraged
to trust in God in chapel and to rely on yourself in the
wider world outside; in chapel, too, you were forced to
listen to stories of the world being created in seven days,
of Noah and his ark and the great flood, of miracles and
virgin births and the dead being raised to life, while in
school you discovered that the universe was thousands
of millions of years old, that the world had never been
drowned by flood waters, and that parthenogenesis was
largely confined to insects. In other ways, however, I
began to see that what went on in chapel and outside it
were not as different as I had hitherto thought them to
be, for in both places you were subject to the same
school rules and discipline, and in both places you were
lectured and expected to attend to what was said or risk
being punished. Meanwhile, what went on in chapel
was no longer so much numinous, if unintelligible, as
boring, hypocritical and nonsensical, so that I listened
only to mock or to be irritated or both. Curiously

enough, I still believed in God at this time, but it was a belief of a primitive, unformulated and fragile nature, and it did not long survive the vigorous materialism of the whole of the rest of my education, which was shot through and through with late nineteenth-century materialism and optimistic humanism.

I was, I think, unpopular at school, and although at the time I could not understand why this should have been so, I am no longer surprised; for in retrospect I can see that I was large, ready to be aggressive when provoked, and addicted to swimming against the stream. I was also bad at games, resentful of authority, and endowed with a dangerous command of words with which it was both easy and often irresistibly enjoyable to sting people. I alienated many of my contemporaries by not conforming to their ideas and conservative ideals while at the same time failing to fit neatly into the accepted nonconformist mould of the time; thus I thoroughly enjoyed running about the downs, naked whenever the weather and the emptiness of the landscape allowed, with my heterosexual, rugger-playing friends, with whom I kept young sparrow hawks and kestrels which we had taken from their nests and tried unsuccessfully to tame and train until such time as they escaped and flew away to fend for themselves; but I also spent as much time as I could in the Art Room with those of my less conventional friends who were classified as 'aesthetes' and who were therefore much distrusted and disliked by the staff. Some of these were homosexual, but since most of us at the time were to a greater or lesser degree bisexual and not in the least particular as to what aroused us erotically, almost anything being sufficient to awaken our loins and fill our heads with dreams, the nature of my friends' tastes in this respect did not seem to me to be important.

Meanwhile, if the other boys found me difficult to classify, with very few exceptions the masters at the school gave the impression of regarding me as an unmitigated disaster, and my taste in painting, poetry and music made things worse. For my first sight of Van Gogh's paintings, though only in reproduction, was almost like the vision given to St Paul on the Damascus road: a revelation of unexpected and surpassing glory. It is difficult today to recall how revolutionary and startling his paintings were in the 1920s, for they have been reproduced and admired for so long that nowadays they are rightly treated with the respect due to masterpieces; but in those far-off days they still had the power to astonish and to shock, so that while they took my breath away and excited me even more, I think, than any blossoming girl in the high street or flowering boy under the shower, almost to a man my mentors considered them ugly vulgar daubs, garish, unskilled and artless. Matters were made worse by the fact that I was equally excited by the discovery of T. S. Eliot's poetry; the *Waste Land* and his 'damp souls of housemaids sprouting at area gates' together with such poems as 'The Love Song of J. Alfred Prufrock' opened up a new vision of the world to me in much the same way as Van Gogh's paintings, though the two worlds revealed were very different from each other; but Eliot, too, was deeply distrusted and disliked by the majority of my teachers, who were convinced that his poems were ugly, absurd, revolutionary and therefore subversive and dangerous. Plainly, I could not really like them or see any value in them, for none existed, and therefore I must be lying with some ulterior motive and expressing an admiration for them as a demonstration of my dumb insolence and rebellious intent. In a way, of course, they were right; for while I genuinely loved Eliot's poetry, as

I still do, I was also delighted that my taste for it gave me an opportunity to offend and annoy as many members of the school staff as possible against whom I did, indeed, feel intensely rebellious and full of insolence, both dumb and sometimes not so dumb. They also disliked my taste in music. As far as I can remember, there was little opportunity to hear much music at school, but as I came from a musically barren family, I may have failed to take what opportunities existed; but at the age of about fifteen or sixteen I became excited by the more way-out jazz of the period, banned at school and heard surreptitiously on a portable gramophone in a water meadow, where the sounds made by such men as Louis Armstrong and Duke Ellington mingled with the cry of coots and the buzzing of insects; and this occupation of mine, too, was regarded as a proof of my depravity.

If the tenor of my life was changed by the impact of the arts, which led back from Eliot through the *Oxford Book of English Verse* to the discovery of a host of other poets, and similarly from Van Gogh to Cézanne, Modigliani, Picasso and Matisse and through them to a great treasury of older masters, it was at about the same time that the subliminal materialism of my education, never openly avowed by my teachers but washing away like a tidal sea at the submerged banks of my being, gradually produced a revelation as stimulating and important as that vouchsafed by Eliot and Van Gogh: namely, that there was no God, and religion was either social hypocrisy or intellectual obscurantism or both. The atheism of men like Bertrand Russell shone out like the light of the sun dispelling not only the darkness of my childhood's innocent night but also the morning mists of my adolescent respect for the solemn and sacred things, which, though unintelligible to me, I had taken on trust from my elders in the belief that they knew more than I did about the mysteries of life. My rejection of the religious odds and ends upon which I had hitherto been force-fed, and my decision to count myself an atheist, not an agnostic, was enormously exhilarating and liberating.

So I avowed myself an atheist, and in doing so I felt that I had emerged from a dim, smoke-filled room, stale and drab and airless, into a bright and bracing world, blue and salty with the smell of sea breezes and as full of light as a Norfolk sky. I was about sixteen at the time, and I had not yet come across the ideas of the logical positivists of the so-called Vienna Circle but I tried to read Nietzsche with, I fear, more enthusiasm than understanding, and I discovered A. N. Whitehead's book, *Adventures of Ideas*, which enraptured me. It was at about this time, too, that I was introduced to that sacred writ of traditional unbelief of the day, *The Thinker's Library*, published by the Rationalist Press Association. To crown it all, as I have already briefly said, I devoured all the simpler and more popular works of that urbane, brilliant and supremely lucid 'idiot's guide' to polite atheism, Bertrand Russell, and the more I read the more convinced I became that I had been right to reject belief in God and become an atheist.

At the time, I was convinced that this decision of mine was an intellectual one taken on purely rational grounds, and so to a certain extent it was; but in retrospect I realize that it was also partly an aesthetic and partly a moral decision: aesthetic because the atheism I embraced at this time was clearer, more economical and more satisfying than the old mixture of vestigial Christianity, covert materialism and optimistic humanism served up with Stoic sauce upon which I had been fed since childhood, and moral because atheism seemed to me to be infinitely more honest and intellectually more courageous than the religion I had been taught at school. Looking back, however, I am sure that I also rejected the version of Christianity which I had hitherto accepted because with it I could reject, too, a number of what seemed to me to be unnecessarily restrictive rules and conventions, together with those people – schoolmasters and others – who had forced them upon me and all that they stood for. In other words, my 'intellectual' decision was also a vehicle for revolt against much else.

However, what the world, my family and I myself were going to do with me as my schooling drew to its welcome if undistinguished close was a problem. To everyone's surprise including my own, I had managed to pass the various examinations which took the place at that time of today's O and A levels, but I was basically uninterested in further academic education, and the idea of sending me to a university never arose: not that going to a university necessarily had anything much to do with further education in those days; the father of three boys I knew sent them all to his own old college at Oxford on the strict understanding that they were not being sent there to do any work, but to 'learn to behave like gentlemen'. My only accomplishment was that I could draw and paint slightly better than most of my contemporaries, and I had won various prizes and cups reserved for boys good at such useless pursuits; so without bothering to refer to my family I decided to enter for a scholarship for the Royal Academy School of Art, not so much with the intention of going there, let alone of becoming a professional artist, as to discover whether I could win a scholarship or not, rather as I might have tried to win a prize in a competition to solve a crossword puzzle. In the event, I got my scholarship, and thus I found myself bound for an art school almost by accident.

I received the news of my success four days after leaving school, and I started work at the RA a few days later, not really knowing my arse from my elbow, as they say, and indeed knowing even less about the fascinating anatomical details of the various ladies who now posed naked for me to draw: a spectacle which, to my surprise, paralysed me for no longer than about three days, after which I found that I could begin to breathe again in their presence at something like the normal rate of respiration despite their almost magical opalescence and beguiling pulchritude.

II

Freedom, Uccello and War

Life as an art student conferred upon me an enormous sense of freedom. In my experience, Wordsworth had been right to say that 'Shades of the prison-house begin to close Upon the growing boy' at a horribly early age, but somehow, miraculously, the prison gates which had begun to close on me at the age of eight had swung open again on leaving school, and I could not agree with the poet that whatever vision had attended me in my youth had now begun inexorably to 'die away, And fade into the light of common day.' On the contrary, life was more exciting than it had ever been, and the vision of the world implicit in my atheism was both liberating and exhilarating: a world not only intellectually more acceptable but also cleaner and brighter than the old, dim, musty world of superstitious bits and pieces which I had left behind. It was a luminous world with no shadows, no muffled edges, no obscure passages or hidden meanings: a world which was potentially intelligible even if there were areas of it which were not yet fully understood. Years later, when I was reading Erich Auerbach's *Mimesis*, in which he said of Homer's poetry and of his world that 'the syntactical connection between part and part is perfectly clear, no contour is blurred ... Clearly outlined, brightly and uniformly illuminated, men and things stand out in a realm where everything is visible; and not less clear — wholly expressed even in their ardour — are the feelings and thoughts of the persons involved', I was immediately reminded of how I had felt in those first heady days of

my bright and salty atheism. Life took on something
like that same Homeric luminosity and clarity for me, as
it had when the Greek sun had warmed and tanned the
limbs of Odysseus, and the wine-dark Aegean sea had
crusted them with salt.

The RA was a small art school; there could not have
been more than fifty students in all, and perhaps fewer
than that, but amongst them some became my lifelong
friends. Mervyn Peake, a brilliant draughtsman and
later to prove an even better writer and poet, remained
my friend until he died after an appalling illness which
reduced him to a doddery old man in what seemed to be
only a few months. The son of a Congregationalist
missionary doctor in China and a bewildered little
mother, he was as full of vitality as a bottle of cham-
pagne is full of bubbles with a zest for living and a rich
imaginative life which I have never seen surpassed. He,
too, had rejected conventional religious belief, presumably in reaction against indoctrination by his parents,
but later he was to write a poem in which something
very like religious faith is implicit.

> To live at all is miracle enough.
> The doom of nations is another thing.
> Here in my hammering blood-pulse is my proof.
>
> Let every painter paint and poet sing
> And all the sons of music ply their trade;
> Machines are weaker than a beetle's wing.
>
> Swung out of sunlight into cosmic shade,
> Come what come may, the imagination's heart
> Is constellation high and can't be weighed.
>
> Nor greed nor fear can tear our faith apart
> When every heart-beat hammers out the proof
> That life is miracle enough.

It is indeed, and curiously enough Bertrand Russell made much the same point, adding another one for good measure; at least, I believe he did, though I have failed to discover where he said it; but I remember reading somewhere his remark to the effect that there are only two real miracles, first that anything exists at all, and secondly that the kettle never freezes when it is put on the fire: that is to say, existence and the universality of natural law.

But, of course, Mervyn Peake was not the only student at the RA, and I made other friends there: Peter Scott, Eileen Guthrie, Arthur Mackenzie, Brenda Streatfeild and others; and it was at this time, too – to indulge in a little name-dropping – that I shared a studio for a while with Dylan Thomas and one or two other people. But it was Mervyn Peake who was responsible for persuading me to go to Sark in the Channel Islands, where an attempt was being made to found a small artists' colony, and I in turn asked Brenda Streatfeild if she would come there with me; after some hesitation, she agreed to do so, and for the next four years we spent the five or six months from about April to September living there together in a barn, painting, bathing and omnivorously reading the classic works of the great English, Russian and French novelists, which could be bought in the Everyman Library in a cloth-bound edition, unbelievably, by today's standards, at two shillings a volume. We were there from 1934 to 1937, and for me it was a time of almost total irresponsibility, freedom and happiness; but as the years passed and more people arrived to join the little group of painters there, the first fine flush of freedom began to pall a little and even to resemble aimlessness. Perhaps I was growing up.

In 1937, Brenda Streatfeild and I got married, and

found somewhere to live in Kent: an old farmhouse
with a garden and a number of out-buildings for which
we paid a pound a week in rent. Brenda was the product
of a family of militant atheists from whom I learned a
great deal; her father was a doctor and the least rational
rationalist I have ever met; immensely kind, fanatically
socialist and anti-Christian, especially anti-Catholic, he
had reacted with splendidly righteous violence against
his rather aristocratic and stuffy background, while her
mother was an odd woman with two children by her
husband – Brenda was one of them – and two by John
Littlewood, the Cambridge mathematician, whose mis-
tress she was for years. A clergyman's daughter, she too
was a passionate atheist, an intimate friend of Bertrand
Russell, and a brilliant pianist. I owe her an incalculable
debt, for I learnt through her how much I had missed by
never hearing classical music; she introduced me to
Beethoven's piano sonatas, to Mozart, Bach, Brahms
and to much else, and this was an experience which
overwhelmed me.

During this period, two occasions remain as memorable as that early childhood day when I picked a purple
and white pansy for a stranger in a white suit on a white
painted bench. As a student at the RA, I often went to
the National Gallery in Trafalgar Square at lunchtime,
there to eat a sandwich or two and look at the pictures.
At that time, Uccello's *Rout of San Romano* hung on a
wall near the main entrance; everyone had to pass it in
order to reach the other galleries further into the building. I had passed it many times, and it did not interest
me; indeed, it seemed wooden, quaint and boring.
Then one day it arrested me – almost knocked me down
– revealing itself to me in a great flowering burst of
balance and delight. No longer wooden, stiff and for-
mal, the figures were poised for action as elegantly as

hovering birds, the whole as rich and colourful as a Persian carpet; even the little man lying dead under the horses' hoofs in full armour with his feet towards the observer and his head pointing in the opposite direction, of whom it was often affectionately said that he had died in the cause of perspective, even he was no longer merely slightly comic, but, with the rest of the picture, he was transformed. It was as if scales had fallen from my eyes, now I could see for the first time. Moreover, it turned out that my eyes had been opened not to the glories of Uccello alone but also to the splendours of the whole world of the early Renaissance in Italy. Thus it was a moment which changed and vastly enriched me and my life.

The other occasion was a little later, after I had left the RA and Brenda and I were living in Kent. For some reason I had gone to London for the day. It was high summer, and I travelled home by train. I found myself in a shabby old suburban carriage with ancient sepia-coloured photographs of seaside resorts such as Margate and Folkestone in Edwardian days flanking a fly-blown mirror on the carriage wall above the seats and a door with a dusty window which could be let down by means of a broad leather strap with holes in it, which one placed over a brass stud to hold the window in the desired position. There was no corridor; I was alone; and as the train reached the Kentish suburbs the evening took on a depth and breathless splendour which was quite unexpected, with the sky fainting away from pale blue to lemon; the air was like that in Van Gogh's picture of the *Restaurant de la Sirène* at Joinville, the landscape filled with a stillness which invaded me like smoke, and the trees heavy and dazzlingly dark in hanging gardens running down to the railway line, while the houses glowed as if they were in paintings by Bonnard. I did not dare move lest I should shatter the vision, disturb the pool of stillness, rupture the membrane enclosing the moment of time as a drop of water encloses a bright bubble of light. I was conscious of myself, too, as I had never been before, of my life within me, the depth and the dynamo-hum of it in the darkness of the circulating blood, and with all this I was sure that I was within a hair's breadth of understanding the meaning of my own existence and that of the phenomenal universe around me; indeed, I knew that I was. But I was not. I am not sure how long the experience lasted, ten minutes perhaps or a little more, and when it died I had discovered no secret; but I had had the experience, and I have never forgotten it.

All this was lived under the lengthening shadow of war. Young men, more dedicated and sure of themselves and the great issues of the day than I was, went to Spain to enlist in the International Brigade against General Franco and his Fascist allies, making me feel slightly guilty for not doing so, and Picasso painted his picture of the carnage wrought by German bombers in the Basque town of Guernica. When it was exhibited in London it greatly impressed me as did the loosely related discovery during these pre-war years of the works of Henry Moore with his marvellous but depersonalized images of man. It was at this time, too, that I discovered the paintings of Braque, Juan Gris, Miro, Paul Klee and the rest, who either banished the human image altogether or distorted it and reduced it to parity with bulls' skulls, guitars, fish, newspapers and clarinets. If artists are the representatives of their society and time, embodying and expressing in their works the deepest self-understanding of their contemporaries, as I believe they are, all this should have terrified me; it did not fit at all comfortably with my inherited humanism with its belief in the supremacy and perfectibility of man and the automatically beneficent nature of progress, though it co-existed happily enough with my atheism. But at the time I did not notice the contradictions let alone worry about them, for they were overshadowed by the rantings of Hitler and Mussolini and by the Japanese invasion of China which continued to go its murderous way. I remember watching a newsreel of bombs spilling like poisonous eggs out of the belly of Japanese aircraft over China, and another of a grinning Japanese soldier in uniform with a bayonet fixed on the end of his rifle indulging in bayonet practice, not on a sack stuffed with straw as was usual, but on a young Chinese man with a face like that of a terrified child, as he waited to be stuck in the stomach by the soldier, while a ring of appalled but impassive spectators watched as the two men circled each other like insects in unequal but mortal combat.

Since most of my schoolmasters, uncles and the other adult men amongst whom I had grown up had lost arms, legs, lungs or minds – those who had survived – between 1914 and 1918, the thought of war appalled me. Apart from being terrifying, it was a failure of everything in which I believed: a failure of humanity, intelligence, love, justice and sanity and at the same time the triumph of bigotry, ignorance and passion over the scientific approach to the solution of human problems, as I then idealistically conceived such an approach; and the one thing my atheism could not cope with was failure. Once again, it was borne in on me how well my school had done, for while it had spoken of faith in God, it had actually taught me self-reliance and had mocked weakness while extolling self-assertive strength and success. The old boys who had become cabinet ministers, bishops, generals or admirals, or those who had risen to great heights in the law or the diplomatic corps were held up to us all as examples and pointed out with pride on prize day. If they could have done so, I suspect that most of the masters of the school and many of those who had survived its rigours as pupils and had subsequently gone from strength to strength in their chosen occupations would have liked to add an eleventh commandment to the Decalogue, and to have inscribed the words 'Thou shalt not fail' on the stony tablets of our juvenile hearts. In fact, whether they had intended to do so or not, they had done just that to me, so that, as the obvious political and social failures of the time led inexorably towards another war, and as I began to become aware of a number of personal failures – failures of relationship, failures as a painter, failures within myself, some of which were trivial but some of which were very far from trifling – I became subject to recurring periods of black gloom and despair.

On the whole, however, these bouts of darkness were short-lived and infrequent, and my atheist paradise remained very much a paradise most of the time, and not for a moment, even in my gloomiest moods, was it troubled by idiotic doubts about the existence of God; at least I was not going to be misled again by that ancient fable. It was a time, too, of the first 'one-man' exhibition of my paintings in a London gallery, of critical success and growing assurance as a painter despite my occasional bouts of despair over individual paintings, and of my first trips abroad. Just before the Civil War there, I had travelled through Spain from Gibraltar and Malaga to Granada, Toledo and Madrid, going from place to place as cheaply as possible by bus, surrounded by Spanish peasants with their chickens and even occasionally their pigs, to worship at the shrines of El Greco, Velazquez and Goya, whose *Disasters of War* cast a terrifying and prophetic light forward on to what was about to happen once again in Spain and a very little later in most of the rest of Europe.

Not long before the Second World War broke out, my brother and I and Brenda and Eileen Guthrie bicycled to Chartres, sleeping in little tents on piles of straw, and delighting the various French farmers upon whose land we asked permission to spend the night by the thought that they were playing a part, however small, in promoting at best a little adultery and, failing that, at least some enjoyable fornication; but since by this time Brenda and I were married, and since Eileen was aware of the fact that, as with mathematics, so with sleeping bags, two into one won't go, the vicarious pleasure of our Gallic hosts in the sexual goings-on of their English guests was founded upon an illusion.

But the sight of Chartres Cathedral, as it appeared in the distance like some great ship riding triumphantly over the cornfields of *la Beauce*, that endless plain over which we pedalled our laborious way from café to café, croissant to croissant, and cup of coffee to glass of wine, was anything but an illusion; and when we reached the city itself and actually approached the cathedral, I was dazzled. Rodin had called it 'the Parthenon of northern Europe', and he was right; for the encrusted splendour of the sculptured figures of the Portail Royal and the other great doorways was at least as exciting in its twelfth- and thirteenth-century way as the carved glory of the Acropolis at Athens must have been before Lord Elgin removed the famous marbles and brought them to London; and the stained glass windows inside the place were even more breathtaking than the sculptures. That first visit to Chartres, with the innocence and excitement of its carefree irresponsibility, before the peace of Europe was finally shattered by tanks and the sun was blotted out by bombers, was the last time the world allowed me to be young; for although I did not know it then, the next time I was destined to enter Chartres Cathedral was three days after war had finally broken out in 1939, when I was returning from a holiday in southern France near Narbonne, and already the glass had been removed for safety; the windows were empty, and the moonlight was streaming into the cathedral, lighting the silence of the nave with the milky and improbable radiance of a dream. I remember wondering how many people would be dead by the end of the war and thinking that it might be as many as five or six million. In the event, sixty million proved to be nearer the mark.

On returning to England I joined the army, as did many of my pacifist contemporaries, for though war was abhorrent, the thought of the triumph of Hitler's Germany was even more so. Indeed, the prospect of the dominance of Nazi policies, beliefs and behaviour over the body politic of the civilized world was as appalling as the thought of the triumph of syphilis or cancer over one's own mortal body. In fact, joining the army after years of increasing anxiety over the possibility of the outbreak of war was a relief; as a private soldier I could no longer do anything for the world (not, of course, that I had ever been able to do so), so I found myself free of both political and personal responsibility for whatever the future might bring, and my days were taken care of by other people. It was a strange kind of haven in the midst of a world in process of violent dissolution, but it had its advantages. For one thing, as I shared my days with the other private soldiers in my platoon, it conferred on me freedom from the middle-class ghetto in which I had been raised; bricklayers and engine-shunters became my friends, and after a little initial embarrassment treated me as such, showing me photographs of their wives and girlfriends, and complaining bitterly at the way the army treated them. It cast an interesting light on my own past that I and two of my fellow recruits, Tony Brett who had been educated at Stowe and Jack Grayburn who had also endured a public-school education, and who was later to be killed at Arnhem and awarded a posthumous VC, were the only people who were not convinced that the army was doing its sadistic best to destroy them; conditions at school had been similar and if anything rather worse than those imposed on us by the army, so that we were comparatively happy, while my engine-shunting friends were not. Socially, it was a richly mixed existence; Tony Brett was the son of the actress Zena Dare, who had a cottage at Ascot not far from the place where he and I and Jack Grayburn were eventually sent to be trained to be officers, and it was in her house that I met Joseph Kennedy, the father of John F. Kennedy, Bobby and Edward. He was the American ambassador to the Court of St James at the time and was convinced that England would lose the war. I did not like him. I much preferred my engine-shunters who had no doubt that he was wrong, and though a commission was soon to reassert the control of the class ghetto upon me bodily, my heart was free once and for all from its lunatic and impoverishing limitations.

As the sky gradually darkens before a summer storm, and a few heavy thundery drops, spaced out and falling as deliberately as ripe apples in autumn, give notice of the coming downpour, so the bombs came. Tentatively, almost shyly at first, they dropped from a dark sky and killed a few luckless people, as German bombers ranged over the country at night virtually unopposed and indulged in a little target practice. A cottage near Zena

Dare's was demolished while her son and I and Ambassador Kennedy sipped her brandy just after the fall of Paris, but it did not greatly disturb us. Before the war everyone had imagined that the effect of bombs on open cities would be so much worse than it actually was at this time that, far from being unnerved by the impact of this first stealthy onslaught, its effect was almost euphoric; but the euphoria did not last long. I was commissioned into the Buffs in September 1940, and I joined the 4th battalion in camp near Ross-on-Wye, where it was waiting to go to Malta. Since, eventually, it was taken there through the Mediterranean by the Royal Navy and shipping space was severely limited, the commanding officer was told to leave the reserve company behind; and since, as the most useless and newest officer, I was eminently dispensable, I was left behind in charge with vague assurances that at some time in the future I should have to bring it out by way of the Cape to join the others. In the meanwhile, I was moved to Plymouth with about a hundred and forty men to await transportation, and it was at Plymouth early in 1941 that I discovered just what bombs could do when they ceased to be shy and began in earnest to produce their crop of corpses. As a junior officer, I was ordered to take a small party of men to help clear up the city after a raid. We dug one old man out of the rubble of a collapsed brick tunnel under the main railway line not far from Plymouth Station, where he had taken shelter; clearing the bricks one by one, the first thing we came across was his pink bald head, fringed with a ruff of white hair and spotted with blood; it was still warm, so we hoped that he might be alive, but he was dead. We took him to a room in the local primary school, which had been pressed into service as an emergency mortuary, and there we laid him on the floor with a number of other corpses. I shall always remember a young woman with a child on either side of her, sitting up with their backs propped against the wall; apart from the fact that they were totally naked, as pale as milk and unnaturally still, there seemed to be nothing wrong with them; but they, too, were dead, killed by blast and stripped in the process. 'Blast does funny things sometimes,' said a jovial man who seemed to be in charge. He was right; later that morning I found what looked like a wig in the wreckage of an aircraft which had crashed during the raid, but when I picked it up it proved to have meat inside; it must have been a scalp which had belonged to one of the crew.

Early in 1941, orders at last came that I was to take the reserve company to Malta. We went by sea in a large convoy which, as was expected, travelled by way of Cape Town, and landed in Egypt on my wedding anniversary, 10 May, just after Crete had fallen to the Germans and the sea route to Malta had thus been blocked. As a result we were labelled 'For Disposal', but in the meanwhile we provided a guard for part of the docks at Alexandria, where I watched the bodies of men killed by German dive bombers over Heraklion harbour being cut out of the tangled wreckage of the ships. The *Orion* had been hit in three places; it took almost three weeks to rid her of bodies and bits of bodies. The smell in the Egyptian sun was appalling as she and her sister ships were cleared of the dead. I never got to Malta, but stayed in Egypt, where for the next two and a half years my life was punctuated by bodies and bits of bodies. I never got used to them. Sometimes the only protection against them was to laugh. On one occasion, one or two friends and I were watching an aerial battle when an Italian airman baled out of his plane as it caught fire, and we saw his parachute begin to split until it became an open-ended cylinder; he plummeted into the ground a hundred yards away, and splashed like an over-ripe fruit. In sheer self-defence against such a sight, the only thing to do was to laugh – at least, that is what we all did – helplessly and feeling sick.

Shortly after arriving in Egypt, my 'disposal' was arranged by attaching me to a small group of people whose task it was to study photographs of enemy-held territory taken from the air, and to gather as much information from them as possible. I knew nothing about the job, but I knew a little about photography, and that was enough for the army, as indeed it was for me, for it was fascinating work. After a few days basic training in the technique of 'reading' stereoscopic photographs, I was sent to join three other people who were doing the job in the Western Desert. I knew from reading Gibbon that the Egyptian desert in the third and fourth centuries had been as full of saints and hermits as a Christmas cake is full of currants, and now that I was there myself I was not surprised that they had chosen to live in its hot and stony wilderness; for while Gibbon had mocked them, and as an atheist I disapproved of them, the desert made it impossible for me not to begin to understand them, and even indeed to share something of their taste for its desolation. It was a place of poverty in the truest sense of complete absence of possessions, things, comforts and frills: indeed, a place conferring on me a sudden freedom which was exhilarating; living there after a lifetime spent in the material clutter of civilization was like emerging at night from the noisy, overcrowded and smoke-filled saloon of a luxury liner on to the deck with no sound but the wind in the rigging and the swish of the sea under a foam of silent stars. The desert might deprive you of all your accustomed securities but, if you were prepared to accept it, it gave you back the unexpected security of a life of minimal demands, in which the self-evident vulnerability of every living thing, especially in time of war, made the fact of being alive at all the one thing that mattered. Like the desert, life was spare, but in its spareness it was both precious and astonishingly beautiful. But, of course, there were times when it was extremely frightening too, as I got tangled up in battles; part of my job was to take information gleaned from the photographs I had studied down to the men doing the fighting, and while their task was incomparably more dangerous than mine, never having been a brave man I found being bombed and shelled and generally assaulted with homicidal intent terrifying. Indeed, I was so frightened at times that I found myself reverting to childish magical rituals to ward off danger, keeping a polished stone in my pocket as a talisman, repeating the Lord's Prayer and knowing that, if I forgot the words in the middle, something awful would happen, or promising to no one and nothing in particular that if I got out of whatever unpleasantness I happened to be enduring at the time, I would get drunk less often, mind my sexual P's and Q's more carefully, or try to be less unkind to the people I disliked. In the event, of course, when the danger was safely past, I would immediately get drunk, take what sexual pleasure I could find, and be particularly bloody to those whom I disliked in an attempt to expiate my self-disgust at succumbing to such superstitious nonsense.

As time passed, and more and more people were needed who could understand the value of the information contained in aerial photographs, I was recalled to Cairo, after about eighteen months in the desert, to join a man named Thornley, a fluent Arabic speaker and a most civilized and charming person, who had lived in

Egypt for years, as an instructor on a series of courses designed to train people to know about photographic intelligence; he had been running these courses single-handed for some time, but could no longer cope on his own. So I hired a room in a *pension* in Heliopolis run by a formidable Armenian woman. One of the other inhabitants, a man of about thirty, had been given an office job by the military police after a very small Italian anti-tank bullet with an enormous muzzle velocity had gone straight through him somewhere near his solar plexus at such a high speed that it had cauterized the wound in the process, emerging and leaving him virtu-ally undamaged: or so he told us. There were one or two girls in the Women's Auxiliary Air Force living there too, one of whom used to come down to breakfast in distractingly inadequate clothes with predictable effects upon the men present; but if any of us made even the smallest advance towards her, she would assume a flinty middle-class expression of disapproval, retreating to her room and making it quite clear that her stainless steel virginity was as impregnable as a bank vault. She moved after a while, and her place was taken by others who were both more friendly and less well-armoured. I got to know one of them very well, spending most of my spare time with her and eventually moving out of the *pension* and sharing a flat with her.

I loved both Egypt and its people. Most British soldiers blamed the unpleasantness of being caught up in a war on the place and its inhabitants, though if they had been there on honeymoon they would have loved both; but in the circumstances they used them as scapegoats, loading all their fears and frustrations upon them, and I was considered both mad and unpatriotic to love Cairo and its people. Some of the latter impressed me by the depth and strength of their Islamic faith; after moving from the *pension* to live in a flat, I had a servant called Mubaraq whose whole life was informed by a kind of matter-of-fact, unpious awareness of God which influenced everything he did, however trivial. I had never met anything like it in a Christian, and while I regarded it as an interesting survival from medieval times and Mubaraq himself as a kind of living fossil rather like a coelacanth, he was impressive nevertheless. So, too, were some of the mosques which I explored in my free time with Frank Scarlett, an architect, and Ben Nicolson, the elder son of Harold Nicolson and Vita Sackville-West and not to be confused with Ben Nicholson, the painter. The great mosque of Ibn Tulun which had been built in about AD 876 seemed to me to be one of the world's great buildings, and En Nasr, built by Mohammed ibn Qalaun in about 1318, was not much less glorious, while the university of El Azhar lived up to its name, The Splendid. There was a quality of openness about these buildings, a simplicity and dignity and spareness, which reminded me of the desert and of Mubaraq's faith in God, and which was in terrible contrast to the tawdry clutter and noisy commercialism of the Church of the Holy Sepulchre in Jerusalem, which I visited later with Ben Nicolson. How much of all this sank down and settled somewhere below the surface of my mind, like rain seeping through to an underground reservoir, I do not know, but I suspect that some of it must have done so. At the time, however, what impressed me even more than the splendours of Islam were the glories of Pharaonic Egypt. I spent two periods of ten days' leave in Luxor, the first with Frank alone and the second with Frank and the girl with whom I was sharing a flat, and the impact of the great temple of Amun at Karnak, the Ramesseum at Thebes and the other great buildings at Deir el Bahari and Medinet

Habu, was overpowering. 'Art is a language,' said Herbert Read, and he was right; certainly the gods of ancient Egypt spoke to me during those visits, even if they did so in a language I did not fully understand and of things I did not wish to contemplate. It was impossible to ignore them.

Late in 1943, after nearly three years in Egypt, I was flown home to join the School of Military Intelligence at Matlock in Derbyshire, there to pass on before the invasion of Europe the knowledge about photographic intelligence gained in the Middle East. I think that some of the foundations of my atheism had already been partly undermined by dead men as well perhaps as by Ibn Tulun and the gods of Egypt; but I had no idea at the time that this was the case and, if it had been put to me, I should have vigorously denied it. I was, I believed, as staunchly atheist as ever, and the sight and sound of bombers in their hundreds against the Derbyshire sky at dusk, as they droned their way eastwards to destroy Dresden or Hamburg or some other German city, did nothing to persuade me that a loving deity was in ultimate command of history.

My first child, a daughter, was born on Christmas morning 1944, and some months later, on 6 August 1945, I was pouring myself a gin and tonic before lunch in the Officers' Mess at Matlock when someone turned on the one o'clock news and I heard that an atomic bomb had been dropped on Hiroshima; apart from a momentary thought that it might have been more humane to have dropped it out to sea or on some paddy fields, having first warned the Japanese to watch its effect, I shared the general feeling of excitement that it probably signalled the end of the war. As everyone knows, it did so, but I was not demobilized from the army until the spring of 1946. Most unexpectedly, the peace, for which in common with everyone else I had been longing for six seemingly endless years, came as something of an anti-climax, flat and lifeless. I returned home to Kent and my paint-box to discover that somewhere along the line I had left behind me, once and for all, the rubble of my youth.

III

The Ford Jabbok

As an old man, Tolstoy said to Maxim Gorky, 'If a man has learned to think, no matter what he may think about, he is always thinking of his own death. All philosophers were like that. And what truth can there be, if there is death?' It is a good question, though I doubt if our own world would agree, for our Western society is profoundly escapist where death is concerned, condemning those who speak of it as morbid, and treating the subject as unmentionable, in much the same way as the Victorians treated sex. People do not die; they depart like trains bound for Portsmouth from platform seven at Waterloo. Yet I do not believe that anyone really succeeds in avoiding all thoughts of death by pretending that it does not exist; at some point in their lives, perhaps at two in the morning when unable to sleep, the fact that the membrane which separates the small warm citadel of their being from the abyss of not being all around them is as thin as cellophane, must inevitably intrude upon them and threaten the false security of their pretence. One day, Tolstoy's question, 'And what truth can there be, if there is death?' has to be faced, and retrospectively I think that as I painted, gardened, played with my children – another daughter had followed the first – read, ate and slept, the bodies of the dead men I had known during the war stirred and began to sprout questions deep down within me. It was all rather like a passage in T. S. Eliot's *Waste Land* which I knew well and loved.

And each man fixed his eyes before his feet,
Flowed up the hill and down King William Street,
To where St Mary Woolnoth kept the hours
With a dead sound on the final stroke of nine.
There I saw one I knew, and stopped him, crying, 'Stetson!
'You who were with me in the ships at Mylae!
'That corpse you planted last year in your garden,
'Has it begun to sprout? Will it bloom this year?
'Or has the sudden frost disturbed its bed?
'Oh keep the Dog far hence, that's friend to man,
'Or with his nails he'll dig it up again.'

I didn't want them dug up again, my corpses, but they
would not lie down or stop mumbling under my breath,
'And what truth can there be, if there is death?' They
did not break the surface of my conscious mind for a
number of years, only grumbled away below it, and
occasionally flitted across my dreams like bats across the
moon.

However, it was by no means only my corpses which
stirred uneasily somewhere deep inside me; other
things rose up, too, with sufficient force actually to
break the surface of my mind and disturb its tranquillity. It was not just that the longed-for peace was boring
and not at all the same as it had been six years previously, but all sorts of little and not so little failures
robbed me of some of the self-confidence I had had
before the war, so that I no longer felt so much like a god
or so sure of myself. Since I was not prepared to admit
this, even to myself, the optimism which had been
natural to me in the old days before the war – and even
during it – died; in order to maintain an outward air of
optimism, I began to wear a fixed grin like that of a
drunk determined to go on enjoying the party even
though beginning to feel a bit sick. Meanwhile, progress
– the concept of Progress with a capital P – which had

been one of my gods, looked middle-aged and dowdy like someone who had done brilliantly at school but who had gone sadly to seed as the years had passed. In fact, all my old gods began to fray round the edges; sub-atomic physics had destroyed the foundations of classi-cal materialism and its happy certitudes; the banish-ment of poverty – anyway, poverty by nineteenth-century or Calcutta or biblical standards – by the Wel-fare State had done wonders, but had failed to usher in paradise; compulsory free education had waved its magic wand over the darkness of the human heart, and nothing much had happened; slums had been cleared, some by bombs, and people still took drugs and mur-dered their wives (or someone else's) or killed them-selves in housing estates with all mod. cons. instead: indeed, they did so rather more frequently in the deper-sonalized sterility of tower blocks and municipal flats than they had in the solidarity of the old slums.

All this was a shock – painful evidence of the failure of a dream – and my post-war disillusionment deepened when I went back to some of the sources of the dream: to some of the books I had read ten years earlier. Winwood Reade's *Martyrdom of Man* led the field, for in it he had prophesied in 1872 that once religion had been destroyed by science, and man had taken control of his own destiny,

the earth, which is now a purgatory, will be made a para-dise, not by idle prayers and supplications but by the efforts of man himself ... Food will then be manufactured in unlimited quantities at trifling expense ... Hunger and starvation will then be unknown ... Population will mightily increase, and the earth will be a garden ... Governments will be conducted with the quietude and regularity of club committees ... Luxuries will be cheapened and made common to all; none will be rich, none poor. Not only will man subdue the forces of evil that are without; he will also subdue those that are within. He will repress the base instincts and propensities which he has inherited from the animals . . . Man will then be perfect; he will be a creator; he will therefore be what the vulgar worship as a god.

I found that terrifying in its mixture of truth and error, and Winwood Reade was by no means the only humanist prophet to have been mocked by events. In similar vein, H. G. Wells, writing as lately as 1926 after the First World War had done enough, one would have thought, to destroy almost anyone's confidence in man's ability to solve all his problems 'with the quietude and regularity of club committees', had concluded his *Short History of the World* by asking, 'Can anyone doubt that presently our race . . . will achieve unity and peace, that it will live, the children of our blood and lives will live, in a world more splendid and more lovely than any palace or garden that we know, going from strength to strength in an ever-widening circle of adventure and achievement?' Although I did not read it until much later, I felt like replying to Wells's rhetorical question in much the same way as did the Australian Professor of Philosophy, John Passmore, in his book on *The Perfectibility of Man* (1972). 'Only too easily,' he replied drily, 'can we doubt whether our children will live in a world more splendid and lovely than any palace or garden that we know. At best they will live in an air-conditioned box, at worst they will not live at all, or will live in a devastated world.' This seemed possible in the fifties too. Indeed, when Wells revised his *Short History* in 1946, he changed the last chapter and replaced it with one entitled, 'Mind at the End of Its Tether'. There he wrote, rather pathetically, that 'homo sapiens in his present form is played out. The stars in their courses have turned against him and he has to give place to some other animal better adapted to face the fate that closes in more and more swiftly upon mankind.'

Reassessment was therefore forced upon me, as it had been forced upon Wells, and as my old certainties died new doubts were born. I was astonished, too, that T. S. Eliot could deny his 'Hippopotamus' written somewhere around 1920.

> At mating time the hippo's voice
> Betrays inflexions hoarse and odd,
> But every week we hear rejoice
> The Church, at being one with God.
>
> The hippopotamus's day
> Is passed in sleep; at night he hunts;
> God works in a mysterious way –
> The Church can sleep and feed at once.
>
> I saw the 'potamus take wing
> Ascending from the damp savannahs,
> And quiring angels round him sing
> The praise of God, in loud hosannas.
>
> Blood of the Lamb shall wash him clean
> And him shall heavenly arms enfold,
> Among the saints he shall be seen
> Performing on a harp of gold.
>
> He shall be washed as white as snow,
> By all the martyred virgins kist,
> While the True Church remains below
> Wrapt in the old miasmal mist.

How could the man who had written that also write

Murder in the Cathedral and the *Four Quartets?* The
question defeated me, though it should not have come
as such a shock as it did, for I had read the *Quartets* in
the desert during the war and loved them without noticing how religious they were; though how I had managed
to be so obtuse I cannot imagine. I was amazed, too, and
irritated by the way in which Graham Greene, whom I
had met once or twice with Mervyn Peake, could continue to espouse, even to flaunt, his Catholicism, and I
could not believe that John Betjeman's high Anglican-
ism was anything but a rather superior pose; and that
irritated me too. But my astonishment reached its peak
as I listened to the celebrated discussion on the radio
between Bertrand Russell and Fr Copplestone on the
existence of God, for it seemed to me that Copplestone
won the argument handsomely; and this did not irritate
me as much as disturb me, shaking the very foundations
upon which much of my thinking was based, and upon
which indeed it had always seemed secure. Further
demolition work in my head took place as I discovered
that science, taking its cue from Heisenberg, had
embraced uncertainty and chance, if not in the place of
immutable laws, at least alongside them, especially in
the sub-atomic world. Indeed, the furniture of my head
was fast crumbling into dust, and the bright notional
world in which I had been sure of everything, including
myself, was beginning to become a place in which I no
longer felt at home; I could not find my way in it any
longer and, worse, I did not know why I was there or
what I was.

For the crumbling of my internal model of the external world inevitably involved a crumbling, too, of my
notional image of myself. In fact, now that peace had
broken out on earth, 'there was war in heaven' as far as I
personally was concerned, and in many ways it was less

endurable than the earthly war had been. Hopelessly to
mix my mythological metaphors, although I had not
murdered my mother, as Orestes had, like him I had
devoted myself so completely and obediently to the
latest and most fashionable of the gods – in his case
Apollo and in mine scientific materialism – that I had
denied some of the darker and more fundamental
forces, which had brought me into being and had thus
offended the older gods. So, like Orestes, I found
myself the prey of the furies, who were welling up from
the depths and harassing me. It was no consolation that
they also seemed to be harassing Western society in
general, chastising it for its *hubris* and blind obedience
to the upstart gods of the twentieth century. I was
beginning to discover what Jung had meant when he
had said that 'the devil, too, was a creature of God. I had
to read up on the devil. He seemed to be highly important after all'; and it infuriated me. For what was mythology doing making more sense of experience than
reason? Yet it seemed to be doing just that, and in the
process helping me to understand some of the powers
that governed me and my world, while filling the
vacuum left by the abdication of the more rational concepts which I had worshipped hitherto. All that was left
of my previous assurance was a derisive smile like that of
the Cheshire cat, while the mocking voice of George
Meredith kept haunting me with the words, 'Ah! what a
dusty answer gets the soul, when hot for certainties in
this our life!' Sod him, I thought, sod him and his smug
reflections! But my paintings became dark and omin-
ous: sad pictures of people in braces and dark trousers
on dimly-lit beaches with pale children and drab women
and a far-off sea; men on the mud banks of rivers with
old walls crumbling away behind them; families, full-
face, unsmiling without much hope; bits of Florence

and Siena, like dead cities, without people in the streets, empty and still; and they were not even very good paintings.

You have to turn somewhere when the furies are after you, so I tried philosophy again, only to find to my dismay that most of the currently accepted philosophers had retreated into the senior common rooms of ancient universities and had turned their subject into a superior sort of word-game, which was not only divorced from everyday life but which stopped short of asking all the important questions posed by being alive at all. They had brushed them aside on the pretext that they were scientifically and linguistically meaningless. As I understood them, they were not merely protesting against the inadequacy of language, 'the intolerable wrestle with words and meanings' as Eliot had described it, but against the validity of certain kinds of inquiry, so that they seemed to be saying that to ask many of the ancient questions, which had engaged the minds of men from the moment they became men – questions which had been posed by philosophers from Socrates to Nietzsche about the meaning and purpose of existence – was little different from asking, 'Why is Australia?' Instead of bothering with such rubbish, philosophers had decided to confine themselves to analysing the results of scientific discovery, while eschewing metaphysics altogether. In retrospect, I think this may have been an unfair judgement on the linguistic philosophers, but I did not think so at the time, and perhaps there was some truth in it; for it was Wittgenstein himself, by far the greatest of them, who said that 'even if all possible scientific questions be answered, the problems of life have not been touched at all.' Moreover, if Wittgenstein's friend and biographer, Malcolm Norman, is to be believed, 'Wittgenstein did not reject the metaphysical; rather, he rejected the possibility of *stating* the metaphysical.' If you do not count poetry and the other arts as 'statements', I am inclined nowadays to agree with that, for as Eliot knew, when put to such service 'words strain, crack and sometimes break, under the burden, under the tension, slip, slide, perish, decay with imprecision, will not stay in place, will not stay still.' They also suffer terribly from use and abuse; even the greatest words – grace, charity, beauty – become shop-soiled and tatty from much mouthing and over-exposure, until eventually they are emptied of their meaning by constant reproduction, as miniature plaster casts of Michelangelo's *Pieta* lining the shelves of tourist shops near St Peter's, Rome, are as dead as the dust they are made of. But at that time the questions I wanted to ask were too pressing for me to be put off by A. J. Ayer and his fellow academics with their fastidious doubts about language, and so I turned instead to older loves for help.

Russell still excited me by his sheer lucidity, but having heard his discussion with Copplestone I was less sure of his infallibility, so I dipped into the works of others, Whitehead again and Collingwood, who drove me back to look at some of the great figures in the fairly recent history of philosophy: Descartes, Kant, Hegel and Nietzsche. I even tried Karl Marx, but I did so with anything but an open mind, for two things prejudiced me against him: if philosophies like religions are to be known by their fruits, then the bitter fruit of Marxist ideas in Stalin's Russia and elsewhere had already filled me with distaste for Marxism, and this was reinforced by my growing disillusionment with the kind of nineteenth-century optimism about human nature upon which Marx seemed to have based his ideas. 'To see the glory of human nature,' wrote his friend Friedrich Engels, 'to understand the development of the human species in history and its irresistible evolution, to realize its always certain victory over the unreasonableness of the individual, we do not have to call in the abstractions of a God to whom we attribute all that is beautiful, great, sublime and truly human.' Phrases like 'the glory of human nature' sounded strange in the aftermath of Buchenwald, Dachau, Treblinka and the other camps, as indeed did 'the always certain victory over the unreasonableness of the individual' after the treatment of individuals by the state in the USSR, Poland, East Germany, Czechoslovakia, Hungary and elsewhere. Far more appealing than this socialist version of Winwood Reade's man-made paradise in cloud-cuckoo-land were the rumours I heard of Søren Kierkegaard. I say 'rumours' for I would not read him; he was a Christian, and that was enough to stop me from doing so; but I allowed myself to read about him, and his emphasis upon the profound insecurity of human existence, upon fear and trembling, and to my astonishment upon the need to doubt all beliefs to the point of despair in order to reach a mature understanding of what being human is all about, spoke to my condition, and to the post-war condition of the Western world, with such aptness that I was impressed in spite of myself.

I was equally impressed in spite of myself, as I paddled in the shallows of philosophy, by how many of the greatest of the philosophers had been theists; plainly, there were far fewer grounds for atheism than I had always believed, and indeed it seemed that intellectually some sort of theism actually made more sense of the evidence than did its antithesis. Of course, since science, with its insistence upon an objective approach to all problems, had gradually replaced theology in the minds of most people as the oracular source of all truth, atheism had become virtually inevitable; for if you embark upon all enquiries having already embraced objectivity as a postulate, you have predetermined that the end of your quest must necessarily be an object or a number of objects; since God by definition is not an object, you have therefore ruled him out of court before setting out in search of him. But up to the time when science began to dethrone theology, some of the greatest minds had affirmed their belief not only in the existence of some sort of God but also in their ability to prove that existence. From Plato and Aristotle through Augustine and Aquinas and Anselm to Descartes, Spinoza and Leibniz this had been true, and this fascinated me without in any way persuading me to agree with them. Similarly, I was fascinated by the so-called 'proofs' of the existence of God without for a moment being coerced into believing that God exists; they delighted me as an abstract intellectual exercise, and perhaps it was not surprising that they should have done so, for even Bertrand Russell in his *History of Western Philosophy* said of Leibniz's presentation of one of them, the so-called ontological argument, that 'although the argument does not, to a modern mind, seem very convincing, it is easier to feel convinced that it is fallacious than it is to find out precisely where the fallacy lies.' But although they did not convince me of the existence of God, the traditional 'proofs' did convince me that it was not unreasonable to believe in some sort of deity; indeed, they convinced me that it might even be more reasonable to do so than not to do so, for, whatever else they might have been, the 'proofs' were eminently reasonable.

Traditionally, there were four of them. The so-called cosmological argument, put at its simplest, starts from the observation that everything in the world, every movement, every change, every event has a cause, and goes on to conclude that therefore there must have been a first cause, a prime mover. The second is somewhat similar; once again at its simplest it begins with the observation of order, pattern and law in the universe, and goes on to conclude that there must be an orderer behind it all, a creator of the observed order and also a final end or goal. The ontological argument, which Russell found so difficult to falsify, is both more abstract and trickier than the previous two; greatly over-simplified, it argues that since the *idea* of God, envisaged by human beings as the most perfect and necessary being possible, undoubtedly exists, and since non-existence would be an imperfection, God must therefore exist. Lastly, the moral argument for the existence of God sets out to prove that God, as the condition of the highest good, must exist, since we know of the existence of lower conditions of goodness, and therefore there must be higher conditions and eventually one that is highest.

Like Russell, I found it impossible to deny that all this was highly reasonable, but nevertheless I found it amusing and enjoyable rather than credible, as indeed I am afraid I found philosophy in general. To me it was an exciting and pleasurable intellectual game with virtually no connection with the real business of living, and from what I could discover it was much the same for many of the philosophers themselves. Wittgenstein was a notable exception, for having decided that philosophy fell short of grappling with all the real 'problems of life', he retired for many years from the philosophical scene in order to lead a life of great simplicity, first as a teacher in Austria, and later as a gardener in a Benedictine monastery where he slept in a toolshed. However, with the exception of a very few others like Kierkegaard and some of the Existentialists, the majority of the philosophers appeared to live lives which were indistinguishable from those of anyone else; and indeed why should they not have done so? I was very far from blaming them, but I was also far from convinced that their philosophy was particularly relevant to the business of living, enjoyable as some of it was to read when one was in the mood for a little esoteric intellectual pleasure. Nevertheless, in retrospect I now realize that I had moved a long way from my original position of convinced atheism, and I was no longer at all sure that to be religious was virtually equivalent to being either obscurantist or stupid or both.

In fact, I was in much the same sort of agnostic position at that time as that described by Bernard Levin in May 1983 in *The Times*, when he wrote that he was 'one of those – and they are many today – who, without any definable set of religious beliefs, yet cannot persuade himself that life is an accident, the universe random, and both without ultimate meaning.' There may have been others, too, who took this view, but I did not know them, though happily my brother was one and my wife was another. Most people seemed rather to agree with Professor G. C. Simpson of Harvard University who said in 1950 that 'evolution turns out to be basically materialistic, with no sign of purpose ... Man is the result of a purposeless and materialistic process that did not have him in mind.' A few took a different view, as did the American scientist and Nobel prize winner, H. J. Muller, who had written in 1943 that he believed that 'purpose is not imported into nature ... It is implicit in the fact of biological organization'; but I had not read his book at the time. Nor had I read Nabokov's *Lolita*, in which my own feelings were even more accurately described by Humbert-Humbert, the ageing and somewhat pathetic paedophile, when he mused,

> Unless it can be proved to me, to me as I am now, today, with my heart and my beard and my putrefaction, that in the infinite run it does not matter a jot that a North-American girl-child named Dolores . . . had been deprived of her childhood by a maniac, unless this can be proven (and if it can, then life is a joke), I see nothing for the treatment of my misery but the melancholy and very local palliative of articulate art. To quote an old poet, 'the moral sense in mortals is the duty We have to pay on mortal sense of beauty.'

Misery was too strong a word for my condition, but my painting was indeed melancholy at this time without being particularly articulate or much of a palliative to my weariness with the struggle going on inside my head; I seemed to have been wrestling with doubts and certainties, fears and failures, hopes and frustrations for years, and I was sick of them. Had I known the book Genesis as well then, or loved it as much as I do now, I should have been jealous of Jacob, who spent no more than one night at the ford Jabbok wrestling with his own problems and fears. I wish I had known it, for it is a marvellous description of a man at the crisis of his life wrestling with his own meaning and destiny.

> And he rose up that night and took his two wives, and his two handmaids, and his eleven children, and passed over the ford of Jabbok. And he took them and sent them over the stream, and sent over that he had. And Jacob was left alone; and there wrestled a man with him until the breaking of the day. And when he saw that he prevailed not against him, he touched the hollow of his thigh; and the hollow of Jacob's thigh was strained, as he wrestled with

him. And he said, Let me go, for the day breaketh. And he said, I will not let thee go, except thou bless me. And he said unto him, What is thy name? And he said, Jacob. And he said, Thy name shall be called Jacob no more, but Israel; for thou hast striven with God and men, and hast prevailed ... And Jacob called the name of the place Peniel; for he said, I have seen God face to face, and my life is preserved. And the sun rose upon him as he passed over Penuel, and he halted upon his thigh.

I was no Jacob, and I did not even know with whom I was wrestling; if anyone had told me that it was God, I should have laughed. But as with Jacob, someone or something had touched the hollow of my thigh during the years of struggle and I was a changed man, even if I did not yet know it. So I, too, halted upon my thigh, and waited for the sunrise.

IV

Advocatus Diaboli

It is easy to over-dramatize things, especially when writing of oneself, and if I have given the impression that I was in a state of unceasing intellectual and spiritual turmoil during the years which followed the war I have misled you. Most of the time I was happy enough. My paintings were exhibited fairly regularly in two of the Cork Street galleries and got good enough reviews; I fell in love with the Byzantines, with Giotto, Modigliani and Matisse; I fell almost equally in love with old-fashioned roses, irises and laced pinks; it was blissful watching our daughters grow up, taking them to Bexhill for holidays, and eventually to a small local school; I rediscovered French literature and devoured the works of Proust, Gide, Stendhal, Alfred de Vigny, Erckmann-Chatrian and others; I took some photographs of churches in Norfolk and in Kent for John Betjeman; and so I could go on. Nevertheless, where atheism had been fine, agnosticism was not. I was unable to tolerate the intellectual vacuum left by the abdication of my old gods. Since science had proved capable of producing both the radioactive shambles of Hiroshima and the equally radioactive isotopes needed for medical research with far from admirable impartiality, I could no longer treat it as the potential saviour of humanity, as I had tended to do before the war; like the god Siva it was both life-giver and destroyer, a god to be feared rather than to be trusted or worshipped. Humanism, in the form in which I had known it, had been based upon the belief that once human beings had the courage to take command of their own fate and command their own destiny, they would build a better and better society, as predicted by Winwood Reade and Karl Marx in their different ways; and as I have already said, as far as I was concerned Buchenwald and Dachau had made that particular belief look so silly that only a lunatic would ever again seriously entertain it. I had never been very interested in politics, and it seemed to me that anyone who thought that the world would be put to rights by politicians must be very bankrupt of hope, especially since the socialist dream had been turned into a nightmare before our eyes as the various Communist regimes in Eastern Europe and elsewhere slaughtered their political opponents apparently without a qualm and Soviet tanks rolled into East Germany, Hungary and later Czechoslovakia. And worst of all, my corpses would not lie down.

Then one day my sister, who did not live far away, asked my wife and me to dinner. Before the remains of the meal had been cleared from the table a group of people arrived for a planned evening of discussion, and we found ourselves trapped into taking part. Amongst the newcomers was a man named Douglas Hill, who was a Cambridge double-first and a priest, while the others were all church-goers. My sister knew perfectly well that I would not have dreamed of attending such a gathering if asked to do so, but knew equally well that I would never refuse an invitation to share a bottle of good claret; and so I found myself seduced into the role of *advocatus diaboli*, arguing the atheist cause and nobly backed by Brenda, my wife, amongst a bunch of supporters of the village church. To our great surprise we thoroughly enjoyed the evening, and it was even more surprising to discover that the other members of the group obviously enjoyed having a couple of atheists in their midst and found our arguments against Christianity both stimulating and interesting, so much so indeed that they did their best to persuade us to come again. They were so friendly and open-minded, so unconcerned to convert us, and so unlike what I had always imagined a bunch of local church people to be, that we agreed to return for more in about a fortnight's time. From then on we became regular attenders at the meetings of this group.

Douglas Hill was a shock to me. I had not come across his like before, having always imagined that most priests conformed to the conventional image of a clergyman so beloved of the writers of comic plays and TV commercials: a faintly idiotic, plum-in-the-mouth, bumbling ass, who blushed if you said 'bother', and spent his time drinking tea with idiotic old ladies. A few clergy are indeed like that but not many, and Douglas was a very different kind of man; urbane, highly intelligent and with a splendid sense of humour, he managed to be both gentle and impressive at the same time, and though he had some fairly obvious faults and limitations I did not discover them until much later. The first thing I learned from him was how little the version of the Christian faith which had filtered through to me at school and elsewhere corresponded to what he said it was. Instead of a heavy emphasis upon stoicism, self-discipline, solemnity and a strict adherence to a legalistic code of restrictive moral precepts, together with much talk of will-power, uprightness, character, stiff upper lips and avoidance of sin, Douglas talked of grace, forgiveness, freedom, love, community and hope; and at the same time he opened up what was for me an entirely new approach to mythology, imagery and symbolism. It was like discovering a new world; I felt much the same as I had when I first 'discovered' Russian literature and when the works of Tolstoy, Dostoevsky, Turgenev, Gorky and the others stretched out before me like a new and splendid continent waiting to be explored, and I was fascinated without in any way being changed in my basic atheistic convictions. Curiously enough, however, Douglas made one remark which had a most memorable effect upon me, even though it was apparently rather irrational and out of character: indeed, at odds with his usual intellectual integrity. I don't remember the exact context, but I think that I must have been extolling the virtues of atheism and atheists when Douglas turned to me and said, 'Yes, I know, but I'd rather be wrong with the angels than right with the atheists.' He said it with an entirely friendly smile and even a kind of self-depreciatory gloss, rather as one might say, 'Oh, yes, I know how marvellous Beethoven is, but I'm afraid I don't like him.' But despite all this, I was shocked into silence, and it was not until some time later that I began to understand what he meant.

For there are two ways of defining 'rightness' and 'wrongness', truth and error, and so far I had come across only one of them. For the Greek mind, the scientific mind and all minds made or pressed into a similar mould, truth is something to be sought intellectually and, when discovered, defined and expressed in a proposition; thus 'being right' is assenting to that proposition. This is a perfectly valid and indeed very important way of envisaging truth, and it has had an enormous influence upon the way in which everyone in Western civilization thinks, upon their outlook on the world, and upon their lives; but it is not the only way of envisaging truth. For minds formed in a Hebraic rather than a Greek mould, truth is not so much something to be sought intellectually as something to be lived: something to be. 'I am the way, the truth, and the life,' said Jesus the Jew, and for Christians at their best it has been more important to lead a fully authentic human life, to *be* true, than to subscribe to a correct intellectual proposition *about* the truth, or about anything else for that matter. Conversely, Christians at their worst have anathematized each other, fought each other, and burnt each other in passionate defence of their own particular doctrinal propositions about what they have chosen to call Christian truth. When Douglas Hill said to me that he preferred to be wrong with the angels than right with the atheists, he was identifying himself in a slightly provocative way with the Hebraic idea of truth at the expense of Greek propositionalism, though of all men he knew perfectly well the value and importance of a rational approach both to intellectual problems and to life itself; in fact, at times he could become quite fierce in defence of those doctrinal propositions about which he felt strongly and considered important.

The impact of Douglas Hill and his group of Christians on both my wife and me was enormous, sending me back to my books in order to fortify and renew my unbelief. Thus there began another long process of internal argument, during which a good deal of my previous ignorance and misapprehension slowly crumbled away until even some of my anti-Christian prejudice also began to disappear; but I still fought a rearguard action against the idea that perhaps my atheism might have been mistaken, and that all those dreary schoolmasters and other tediously pious types whom I had so much enjoyed shocking whenever possible might have been right after all. I was not as sure of the grounds of my atheism as I had once been, but I was as determined as I had ever been not to believe in God if I could help it, let alone become a Christian.

But then, after many months, I woke up one morning to discover that something had happened in my head; a very slight shift in the angle at which I viewed things had somehow taken place, and the fact that this had happened in my sleep entirely without my volition paralysed me with dismay. It was a moment like that in early childhood when I had picked that memorable purple and white pansy, and like that other time on the train in the Kentish suburbs when the world had become transparent and as charged with meaning as a Beethoven quartet, and I knew that I could do nothing about it. I remember the pattern of morning sunlight on the white painted window-frame opposite my bed and on the low uneven ceiling above it, and the faint smell of musk roses and grass coming in from the garden outside as I discovered that I could no longer argue against Christian belief – or anyway the heart of it – but knew that it held some sort of truth, though almost literally God knew what. I knew that I believed almost nothing, but I knew too that I believed something, and I was appalled. I began to sweat and was quite unable to get out of bed. I wanted to run away from myself, from the room, the house, the country, and hide somewhere where I could pretend that nothing had happened. I tried to persuade myself that I was still comfortably, blissfully, serenely and surely atheist; but it was no good. Eventually, I got up in the hope that if I immersed myself in activity – painting, gardening, anything – the feeling would go away, and life would return to normal; but of course it didn't. I am not sure whether I told Brenda about it or not; something a little similar had happened to her some time earlier, but I don't think I dared tell even her, and certainly I kept it a secret from everyone else as if I had contracted syphilis. But as one slowly gets one's breath back after a shock, so as time passed I began to get my mental breath back, and my horror at what had happened began very slowly to fade away. But it was a long time before I felt normal again.

V

Balaam in Moab

Religious experience is suspect. The Church plays it down and has always viewed people making claims to such experience with grave suspicion. This was so even in the so-called ages of faith, when credulity in such matters was much more widespread than it is today. To give only one example from the past: when a peasant named Peter Bartholomew sought an interview with the Bishop of Le Puy and Raymond of Toulouse just after the capture of Antioch by the men of the First Crusade in AD 1098, saying that he had had a miraculous visitation from St Andrew, who had shown him where the spear which had pierced Christ's side on the Cross was to be found, the Count of Toulouse believed him without hesitation as did most of his men, but the Bishop did not; and this was typical. Then, as now, ordinary men and women were much more ready than the Church to listen to those who claimed to have had various kinds of religious experience, and this, I think, in many ways is to the Church's eternal credit. Today's equivalents of Raymond of Toulouse and the rank-and-file Crusaders who put their unquestioning trust in Peter Bartholomew are not so ubiquitous as they were in Crusading days, but nevertheless they are not difficult to find. There are plenty of people, to quote from an article by my friend Professor David Martin, who 'mooch around a fairground of faiths until they find the booth which meets their need. In one booth they may be raised to higher consciousness, in another they can commune with the still music of the plant world, in another dance their sorrows away and uncurl their tight psyches, in another pay obeisance to a guru with an esoteric technique and an oriental vocabulary; in yet another scream away their personal fantasies at each other.' Most of these arcane pursuits are harmless enough, and their popularity may well be laid at the Church's door; for the Church is often so active – indeed, activist – that it seems to have forgotten the virtues of silence, and people in search of a reason for living are driven to look elsewhere. But there are other forms of religious experience which are not so harmless, as was made only too obvious when an American revivalist led an entire congregation of so-called converts to Guyana not so long ago, and there persuaded them to take part in a mass suicide. As Dr Emilio Castro said at the time, this should warn everyone against 'human conversion through the intensity of emotion experienced ... Psychology helps us understand the control techniques of the human mind which have been developed by sectarian religions. Psycho-social studies reveal the mechanism of submission of the personality. This manipulation of mass psychology or of the individual is a well-known temptation to every charismatic Christian leader.' Equally well-known to every parish priest are the people who come to him with patently dotty claims to special relationships with God or revelations from him, which would lie better on psychiatrists' desks than on vicarage tables. Once again, to give one example only, albeit an extreme one: when I was a parish priest in London a young woman on a bicycle came to my house and asked to speak to me. I took her into my study, whereupon she told me that I could sit down if I wanted to do so; it would not be blasphemous on my part, even though she was really the Virgin Mary. She was, she told me, pregnant with Christ but unable to deliver him because her brother had an evil foot in Crewe. She had been to her doctor, who was really John the Baptist, but he had been no help at all, and would I please do something about it. It was difficult to know exactly what I could do, but I encouraged her to go and see a psychiatrist, who happened also to be a priest and a friend of mine. In the event, however, she did not do so.

Nevertheless St John's advice not to 'believe every spirit, but test the spirits whether they be of God', combining as it does a right and proper scepticism with the possibility that some experiences labelled 'religious' may conceivably be genuine and not psychopathic, is worth following. For there can be absolutely no doubt that all religions are based on claims made by their founding fathers to religious experiences and religious revelations, and there is no *a priori* reason to believe that while some such experiences and revelations were real enough in the old days they cannot possibly be so today; you may deny the possibility of religious experience at any time, but you cannot refuse to acknowledge its possibility in one age while acknowledging it in another. Of course, whatever the Church may do in practice, theoretically it does not disallow the possibility of religious experience in any age; but when it allows such a thing to be possible it tends to go on and say to people claiming to have had religious experiences that they are basically unimportant. Instead, great emphasis is laid upon perseverance, discipline and a rule of life. If as a result worship becomes drier, emptier and more boring, never mind! It is dogged endurance that counts. If a marriage dies on its feet, never mind! The couple are joined together eternally by that sacred scrap of paper, a marriage certificate, and it is maintaining a façade of unity which matters. If prayer becomes a penance, never mind! Just get on with it. Thus legalism triumphs, and people get so bored that they either give the whole thing up or desert the Church for one of Professor Martin's 'booths', and who can blame them?

However, there are other forms of experience which, though not religious in the narrow sense of the word, may be relevant to the subject. As I have briefly mentioned, Arthur Koestler has argued that we live our lives on two stages, not one, as Shakespeare would have had us believe in his celebrated lines from *As You Like It*:

> All the world's a stage,
> And all the men and women merely players;
> They have their exits and their entrances,
> And one man in his time plays many parts . . .

Most of those parts, Koestler has argued, are played on the trivial plane of existence, the daily stage upon which we gossip, commute, work, do the crossword, read the paper and watch television; but occasionally, perhaps in the face of death or in the depth of love, or when listening to music, or when swallowed up by what Freud called the 'oceanic feeling', we fall, as through a stage trap-door, on to the absolute or tragic level of experience, and there we view the world in a radically different perspective; returned once more to the trivial level of everyday life, we write off our experience on the tragic level as the result of over-strained nerves. But is it? Often, probably, yes. But it is on this tragic level that occasionally we experience moments of illumination, disclosures, sudden flashes of insight into the solution of problems which have been bothering us; and the lustre of respectability has been conferred upon such moments by the fact that the biographies of eminent scientists are peppered with accounts of ideas coming to them in such moments of unexpected and unpredictable disclosure. T. S. Kuhn in his book, *The Structure of Scientific Revolutions* (1962), has pointed out how accepted scientific ideas are subject to periodical crises, 'and these are terminated, not by deliberation and interpretation, but by a relatively sudden and unstructured event ... Scientists often speak of "the scales falling from their eyes" or "the lightning flash" that "inundates" a previously obscure puzzle, enabling its components to be seen in a new way that for the first time permits its solution. On other occasions the relevant illumination comes in sleep. No ordinary sense of the term "interpretation" fits these flashes of intuition through which a new paradigm is born.'

One of the most celebrated and dramatic examples of such a moment of illumination – such a disclosure – was that experienced by Otto Loewi, the Professor of Pharmacology at the University of Graz. He had been puzzling for a long time over the mechanism by which nerves affect muscles; one night he woke up with a brilliant idea, and reaching for a piece of paper he jotted down a few notes. In the morning he found to his dismay that they were illegible, while he had completely forgotten the idea which had come to him so vividly a few hours previously. All day he struggled to recall it, but it refused to come back. He went to bed depressed; then in the middle of the night he woke again with the same flash of inspiration – the same clue to the problem – and this time he wrote it down with great care. In the morning, when he checked it, he found that it was indeed the vital clue to the understanding of the process of chemical intermediation, not only between nerves and muscles and the glands they affect, but also between the nervous elements themselves; and startling as such a story may be, the biographies of scientists are full of similar tales. 'I can remember the very spot on the road, whilst in my carriage, when to my joy the solution occurred to me,' wrote Charles Darwin of the moment when the idea that natural selection was responsible for the origin and development of species came to him in a flash and changed the course of science and human thinking. Like Otto Loewi, it was in his sleep that Kekulé dreamed of the benzene ring, while Semelweiss's discovery of the cause of childbed fever, Kepler's idea about the elliptical orbit of the planets round the sun, Pasteur's discovery of the cause of anthrax, Einstein's famous intuition which led him to formulate the theory of relativity and hundreds of other discoveries and clues to the solutions of intractable scientific problems are on record as 'coming' to the investigators in moments of illumination. It is no wonder that Professor Hawkinge of Cambridge said recently on television that the one thing necessary to become a good physicist was to have the ability to make intuitive leaps. Roger Penrose, Professor of Mathematics at Oxford and the inventor of a new, post-Einsteinian, six-dimensional space, which he calls 'twister space', has emphasized even more strongly the central part played in creative science by intuition and the authoritative place of aesthetic satisfaction in the acceptability of mathematical theory.

This is not the only aspect of scientific creativity which is very different from the popular idea of the way in which scientists work; they also often grapple with their problems in a far less intellectually articulate manner than is generally supposed. In a survey made amongst American mathematicians by Jacques Hadamard in 1945 entitled *The Psychology of Invention in the Mathematical Field*, all but two of the people consulted said that they did not approach their problems in words or even in mathematical symbols but in a vague way which relied more on visual images than on reasoning; in fact, they felt their way towards a solution, rather as painters explore the visual imagery of their subjects, instead of following a well-lit intellectual path. Einstein was typical when he confessed that 'the words of the language as they are written or spoken do not seem to play any role in the mechanism of my thought . . . which relies on more or less clear images of a visual and some of a muscular type.' Similarly, R. S. Woodworth said that 'often we have to get away from speech to think clearly'. Moreover, as in the process of creating a work of art, the guide in this non-verbal process of groping for solutions to scientific problems is more often aesthetic than rational. The French mathematician, Raymond Poincarré, described it as 'the feeling of mathematical beauty, or the harmony of numbers, of forms, of geometric elegance', and added that 'this is a true aesthetic feeling that all mathematicians know.' He was echoed by the Cambridge mathematician, G. H. Hardy, who claimed in his book, *A Mathematician's Apology* (1940), that such a feeling for beauty was not only the mathematician's guide in his search for solutions to his problems but also the first test of the validity of those solutions when they came to him in moments of illumination. 'Beauty is the first test,' he said; 'there is no permanent place in the world for ugly mathematics.' After that first test, of course, a solution to a mathematical problem, like any other suggested solution to a problem in science, is subjected to as many rigorous experimental tests as can be devised, and these are crucial. But even so, Paul Dirac, one of the greatest of twentieth-century English physicists, has said flatly that in his opinion 'it is more important to have beauty in one's equations than to have them fit experiment.'

But if creative scientists rely more upon moments of

illumination and flashes of inspiration and are guided more by aesthetic considerations than is often supposed by non-scientists and even perhaps by those engaged in what T. S. Kuhn called 'normal science' as opposed to the creative variety, then plainly they are also much closer to the creative artists of this world than most people suppose too; for the artists are the people above all who rely upon moments of illumination for their starting points. Plato spoke for them all when he said that 'all good poets, epic as well as lyric, compose their poems not by art, but because they are inspired and possessed . . . For the poet is a light and winged and holy thing, and there is no invention in him until he has been inspired.' Twenty-four centuries after Plato's time, the Irish poet A.E. said much the same thing in a slightly different way: 'The poetry itself breaks in upon and deflects the normal current of consciousness.' For Wordsworth, it was the transcendent significance of 'the common face of nature' which broke in upon the normal current of his consciousness:

> I felt
> Gleams like the flashing of a shield; the earth
> And common face of nature spake to me
> Rememberable things.

While for Vincent Van Gogh the vision was much the same. 'I really do not know how I paint,' he wrote in a letter which is worth quoting at some length.

Armed with a white panel, I take up a position in front of the spot that interests me, contemplate what lies before me, and say to myself, 'That white panel must be turned into something.' Dissatisfied with my work I return home, put my panel out of sight, and after taking a little rest go back to my work, almost with qualms, to see what it looks like. But even then I am not yet satisfied, for glorious Nature is still too vividly stamped upon my mind. Nevertheless I find in my work a certain reverberation of that which fascinated me. I know that Nature told me something, that she spoke to me, and that I took down her message in shorthand ... and this is never in a tame or conventional language that did not spring from Nature herself.

Echoing Van Gogh, his contemporary Paul Cézanne, writing to Émile Bernard in May 1904 about 'the spectacle that *Pater Omnipotens Aeterne Deus* spreads out before our eyes', told his friend that he was 'progressing very slowly, for nature reveals herself to me in very complex forms, and the progress needed is incessant.'

Beethoven told Louis Schlösser, a musician from Darmstadt:

I carry my thoughts about with me for a long time, often for a very long time, before writing them down ... I change many things, discard others and try again and again until I am satisfied; then in my head I begin to elaborate the work ... It rises, grows up, I hear and see the image in front of me from every angle, and only the labour of writing it down remains ... You may ask where I obtain my ideas. I cannot answer this with any certainty: they come unevoked, spontaneously or unspontaneously; I could grasp them with my hands in the open air, in the woods, while walking, in the stillness of the night, at early morning, stimulated by those moods which with poets turn into words, into tones with me, which resound, roar and rage until at last they stand before me in the form of notes ...

'The earth and common face of nature spake to me' ...

'I know that Nature told me something, spoke to me' . . .
'Nature reveals herself to me' . . . 'My ideas come
unevoked, spontaneously' . . . 'I could grasp them in my
hands.' The emphasis upon disclosure to the artist is the
same, and I could quote many others to similar effect if
space allowed me to do so. 'Reason must trust these
intuitions of the heart,' said Blaise Pascal in yet another
sphere of human experience, and indeed it must if the
arts of mankind are not to be written off as delusory
things: charming confections designed to put a gloss on
the real face of the world, which is in hard fact merely an
insignificant ball of rock. But reason must also trust
those very similar experiences of divine self-disclosure
to such men as Moses, Isaiah, Jeremiah, St Paul and
indeed many others outside the Judaeo–Christian tradition, if religion is not also to be written off with the
arts as expedient but delusory nonsense. To confine
myself to that tradition for a moment, the stories of
Moses and the burning bush, of Isaiah's vision of 'the
Lord sitting upon a throne, high and lifted up, and his
train filled the temple . . . and the foundations of the
threshold were moved at the voice of him that cried, and
the house was filled with smoke', are too well known to
repeat in detail here; as indeed are St Paul's vision on
the Damascus road and the experience he described to
the Church in Corinth, when, 'whether in the body, or
out of the body, I know not; God knoweth', he was
'caught up even to the third heaven . . . and heard
unspeakable words, which it is not lawful for a man to
utter'. But as in the experience of both scientists and
artists, the men involved in these religious experiences –
Moses, Isaiah, St Paul – are passive; they take no initiative, but something is disclosed to them 'out of the blue',
and as Koestler has said of such an experience, although
it is often as 'verbally incommunicable as the feeling

aroused by a piano concerto . . . its primary mark is the sensation that it is more real than any other thing one has experienced before; that for the first time the veil has fallen and one is in touch with "real reality", the hidden order of things, the X-ray texture of the world, normally obscured by layers of irrelevancy.'

Although it may seem arrogant to compare the experiences of such men as Einstein, Van Gogh and St Paul with those of ordinary men and women, I must risk doing so, for I do not believe that there is any essential difference between St Paul's vision on the Damascus road and that which I received when my eyes were opened to the splendour of Uccello's *Battle of San Romano*; though, of course, there was an immense difference in both subject and degree. I would go further and put in the same class the moments when, as a child, I picked that unforgettable pansy and the time, just before the war in that suburban train, when the world grew transparent to the glory of its own essential being, even though they did not change the course of my life at the time; and such moments are experienced by ordinary men and women more often perhaps than most people think. Here is one example recounted to me by a friend:

The winter was exceptionally cold, and many of the schools had to close down for weeks on end, so it was by no means unusual for me at the age of eleven to spend most days playing with my sledge in the snow. I emphasize the point that it was not unusual for me to spend a day that way, for on one particular morning something very strange happened to me, which was to change me for the rest of my life. As I was pulling my sledge up the hill opposite our house, I began to feel quite different. I became acutely aware of the incredible beauty of the morning; the sun was brilliant, the sky very blue and the snow

dazzlingly white and clean. I stopped and looked up into
the sky and felt aware of myself in a way I had never known
before. That moment was mine; everything was unutter-
ably lovely. I longed to be able to share it with the other
children, but when I got to the top of the hill, I knew that
they would not understand; it hadn't happened to them. I
wanted to go home and tell my mother, because by then I
had realized that it was a most important event in my life,
but I knew that she would not understand either, and I felt
different and sad not to be able to share it. It is still very
difficult to describe or explain what happened; words are
quite inadequate; and yet it did change me. I have always
remembered it, and nothing has ever been quite the same
since.

The nineteenth-century writer, Mark Rutherford, had
a similar experience, and he too knew that those to
whom such a thing had not happened would not understand him if he spoke about it.

All my life I had been a lover of the country, and had
believed, if that is the right word, that the same thought,
spirit, life, God, which was in everything I beheld, was
also in me. But my creed had been taken over from books;
it was accepted as an intellectual proposition. Most of us
are satisfied with this kind of belief, and even call it
religion. We are more content the more definite the object
becomes, no matter whether or not it is in any intimate
relationship with us, and we do not see that the moment
God can be named he ceases to be God. One morning,
when I was in the wood, something happened which was
nothing less than the transformation of myself and the
world, although I 'believed' nothing new. I was looking at
a great, spreading oak. The first tinge from the greenish-
yellow buds was just visible. It seemed to be no longer a
tree away from me and apart from me. The enclosing
barriers of consciousness were removed and the text came

into my mind, *Thou in me and I in thee*. The distinction of
self and not-self was an illusion. I could feel the rising sap;
in me also sprang the fountain of life up-rushing from its
roots, and the joy of its outbreak at the extremity of each
twig right up to the summit was my own: that which kept
me apart was nothing. I do not argue; I cannot explain it;
it will be easy to prove me absurd, but nothing can shake
me. *Thou in me and I in thee*. Death! What is death? There
is no death: *in thee* it is impossible, absurd.

I must not quote too many examples of this kind of
thing, but perhaps one or two more are permissible; for
Sir Alister Hardy, who was Linacre Professor of Zool-
ogy in the University of Oxford until 1961 and Professor
Emeritus since then, made a study of this kind of near-
religious experience, and one or two of the examples he
quotes in his book *The Spiritual Nature of Man* (1979)
are memorable. Here are three.

When I was on holiday, aged about 17, I glanced down and
watched an ant striving to drag a bit of twig through a
patch of sun on a wall in a graveyard by a Greek church,
while chanting came from within the white building. The
feeling aroused in me was quite unanticipated, welling up
from some great depth, and essentially timeless.

The second is a little longer.

I spent a week by myself in the cottage when I was fifty
years old. During that week I experienced insights and
inner flights of consciousness that would have been impossible to undergo in any other circumstances. The
aloneness, the changing weather, and the grandeur of the
hillside and hurrying cloud so impressed my mind that my
thought took flight. The turmoil of my mind was sub-
dued, and my life rested in tranquillity . . . I was alone in
retreat for a brief spell, reunited with a nature of heart-
break and searing beauty. I climbed the hill towards the

sea, mindful of my fifty years, conscious of my intellect confounded, and myself a broken reed. Yet aware, so poignantly aware, of a reality which bound me to truth, and locked me in unity with all life. In the moment of revelation there is no past and no future, and it seemed my life was welded into one whole present as I leant against the salty sea wind.

The last one is from Julian Huxley.

I felt mystically united with nature ... for a moment I *became*, in some transcendental way, the universe.

Some people will argue that these experiences are not religious at all, but I think that this would be a mistake. I agree with Professor C. C. J. Webb, who said in his book, *Religious Experience* (1945), 'There is a serious danger of overlooking the existence of a genuine religious experience which, although taking forms less striking and strange [i.e. than those of some mystics], is not therefore less real and significant.' And this remains true, I think, even though not every such experience bears discernible fruit or results in a scientific, artistic or religious 'breakthrough'; but a sufficient number do precisely that for a claim to be made that they constitute, if not a link between science, art and religion, at least a factor which is common to moments of great creativity and originality in all three fields. In all three, too, the experience seems to impose upon the scientist, artist or prophet a compulsion to be faithful to what has been disclosed – to the revelation – and, whatever the cost may be, not to deny it. The *locus classicus* is to be found in the biblical account of the part played by the prophet Balaam during the invasion of Moab by the Hebrew peoples. He was employed by one of their enemies to curse them, but instead he blessed them to the understandable fury of his employer, who threatened to withhold the payment he had promised; but Balaam replied, 'Have I any power to speak anything? The word that God puts in my mouth, that shall I speak.' In a quite remarkable parallel bridging the millennia, John Betjeman, in an interview on television, having said he believed that there was such a thing as a Muse, went on to say, 'I regard myself as not writing my own verse, but as a sieve, through which things come, and I hope to sort them out so that people can understand them; but sometimes a thing presses down, and you've got to do it.' In a somewhat similar vein, Beethoven, speaking to Karl Czerny, the pianist and composer who had been his pupil between the ages of nine and twelve, said on one occasion, 'I have never dreamed of writing for fame and honour. What weighs on my heart must come out, and that's why I have written.'

This sense of compulsion, this conviction that something is being said through you and that it must be said at all costs has been behind the courage of the scientists, artists and prophets who have braved the wrath of their conservative colleagues and defied the public opinion of their day; and there have been many of them. In the scientific world the persecution of Galileo set the tone for the treatment of unwary innovators, but it has not always been the Church which has led the hunt; T. S. Kuhn has pointed out that scientists themselves can be as conservative as medieval Popes when they see the foundations of their accepted scientific models or paradigms challenged by new concepts, rounding on their heretical sponsors with almost as much venom as that once considered typical of Inquisitors. Moreover, the persecuted have become the persecutors from time to time, as when Galileo himself indignantly rejected

Kepler's idea that ocean tides were caused by the moon. Pasteur was violently attacked by the scientific establishment of his day, though he also had a few allies, and the history of science is full of examples of other great innovators being greeted with hostility and incomprehension.

Meanwhile, in the art world, great originality has fared no better; as everyone knows, the French Impressionists were regarded as either mad or deliberately offensive for years, while Van Gogh virtually never sold a painting except to his brother Theo, and Cézanne was left alone with hardly a flicker of appreciation or recognition until he was an old man; and even then very few people saw anything in his works. In the literary world, too, some writers have discovered that they need the courage of a Balaam if they are to be true to their convictions and compulsions; in our own day, Solzhenitsyn is one obvious example. I cannot make up my mind whether it is more amusing or more depressing to observe in conclusion that all this is so well-known today that conformity in the art world consists of being 'original' at all costs, thus turning innovation into the essence of submission to the establishment, and I suspect that the real innovators today are those whose works do not shriek aloud, 'Look how unlike anything else I am!'

If it seems far-fetched to claim that such disclosure-experiences as I have tried to describe (I am wary of the word 'revelations'; it has been devalued by too much use and abuse) constitute links between the apparently very different realms of art, science and religion, it is worth reinforcing that claim by pointing out that two other characteristics are common to all three: a belief in order or harmony and a refusal to despise the ordinary and trivial things of life. All science depends upon a belief that there are laws which, once discovered, explain the behaviour of whatever it is which is being studied (this is true even in the sub-atomic world, although there the laws of chance and probability appear to reign); and these laws are assumed, doubtless correctly, to be constant throughout the universe. Thus it is assumed that the light from a star X million light years distant from the earth, when analysed spectroscopically, will reveal the chemistry of the star, since its various constituents will behave in the same way as similar substances behave in the laboratory; though, of course, there is no possible way of proving this by demonstration. As to the ordinary and trivial things of life, science treats all of them from the fall of an apple to the growth of a mould named *penicillium notatum* in a laboratory as of potential interest and importance. Meanwhile, every work of art in whatever medium – poetry, music, painting or architecture – is an affirmation that order, harmony, balance and design are there for those with eyes to see them. The difference between a landscape of Mont Sainte-Victoire by Cézanne and a photograph of the same bit of country is that, whereas the photograph records the superficial accidents of the countryside, Cézanne's painting is a statement about the underlying structure and harmony in and beyond the land with its trees and rocks and forms against the blue of the Provençal sky; it is a statement which challenges the beholder to agree or disagree that the world is such an ordered and harmonious place and not just an unordered jumble of rock and vegetation; and every work of art makes a similar challenge, though works of different schools embody and express different kinds of order and harmony. As to artists' interest in the ordinary and trivial things of this world, it hardly needs demonstrating; painters in ancient Egypt decorated walls with paintings

of geese, reeds, and slaves; a Minoan craftsman working
in Crete in about 1500 BC made a gold pendant in the
shape of a pair of common wasps or bees and a ball of
pollen to hang round the neck of one of the bare-
breasted ladies of that mysterious and fascinating civilization which centred on the court of King Minos;
Velazquez treated the dwarfs who were the clowns of
the Spanish court with dignity and complete seriousness; Chardin painted pots and pans, loaves of bread
and white tablecloths as though they were as valuable
and as lovely as the treasure of the Incas; and Picasso
picked up discarded pieces of an old bicycle on a rubbish
dump and made them into a bull's head. Lastly, all
religions depend upon a belief that the world is underpinned by a divine order and upheld by a divine plan,
while the intrinsic value of the commonplace creatures
and things of life is a tenet of most of the world's great
faiths. 'Are not five sparrows sold for two farthings, but
not one is forgotten in the sight of God' would make a
motto equally appropriate to scientists, artists and
members of the world's great religions, however often
some of them might fail to live up to its precept.

When all this has been said, however, it should also be
stated that most normal scientific work, most normal
artistic production and most everyday religious practice, though often the long-term result of insights and
inspirations gained in moments of disclosure, are not
directly concerned with such moments or with falling
through Koestler's trap-door, but much more often
with the intellectual analysis or the working-out of
whatever has been experienced there, sometimes by
other people. And this is right and proper; for as Otto
Loewi, when he awoke, checked the validity of the
solution which had come to him in his sleep, subjecting
it to intellectual analysis and experimental tests, so

should every work of art claiming to be inspired be open to a rigorous criticism, and every religious revelation be subjected to an equally rigorous intellectual examination before being accepted; disclosure must be consonant with lucidity, even though on occasion it may transcend it, as it certainly does in great works of art and some mystical experiences. As I have already said, it is especially necessary to put religious claims of inspiration and revelation to the test of lucidity for the simple reason that it is only too easy for legions of slightly dotty people to believe that their lives have been illuminated by blinding flashes of divine light, whereas in fact they have been dimly lit by the *ignis fatuus* of religious delusion born of neurosis; and this is no good either for them or for other people.

Not all of this filtered through to me at the time I have been describing, when I was forced to admit to myself that I was no longer atheist; for instance, Professor Hardy's book was not published until 1979; enough, however, reached me to encourage me to re-examine the foundations upon which I had tried to build an understanding of the world and myself. But I still felt naked and helpless as the shelter of my atheism crumbled around me, and I soon discovered that I could not live for long in the open with the winds of uncertainty and ignorance whistling round my ears. Moreover, the corpses planted in the now deserted garden of my youthful twenties were still stirring and posing the final question that really mattered, namely, What is a man? Gauguin had painted a picture of a dark-skinned girl lying naked on a bed against a strange, exotic and rather frightening background, and he had entitled it, '*D'où venons nous? Que sommes nous? Où allons nous?*' It hung in the Tate Gallery, and it haunted me; but the answers to those questions eluded me.

VI

What Is Man?

Somewhere between two and three thousand years ago, a Hebrew poet addressed his God and said, 'When I consider the heavens, the work of thy fingers, the sun and the moon and the stars, which thou hast ordained, what is man that thou art mindful of him?' It is a good question, and despite its antiquity it is as relevant today as it ever was, even though I suspect that some of the linguistic philosophers might dismiss it as unanswerable and therefore meaningless. Perhaps I malign them, but, be that as it may, I prefer the advice of Socrates in the *Phaedo*; discussing the problem of the immortality of the soul – that is to say, the destiny of a human being – and combining a thoroughly sceptical approach with an emphasis upon the need to choose, he says,

> Problems like that are such that in this life it is extremely difficult, if not impossible, to find out the answer for certain. Nevertheless it is cowardice, weakness and laziness not to investigate from every possible angle the theories and arguments put forward about it, and not to go on doing so until one drops from fatigue. If one does pursue the matter as one should, one is bound to achieve one of two results: either one finds out the true answer, or if this is impossible, one finds the best available human hypothesis, that is to say, the hardest to falsify. That hypothesis one can use as a raft on which to ride the stormy seas of life; assuming, that is, that one cannot find any surer vehicle, that is, some divine *logos*.

But though it is a good question, contemporary man

tends to give it a very dusty answer. For the reality of our situation is that, as a result of the Big Bang some thousands of millions of years ago, there are at least a hundred million galaxies littering the enormity of space and probably many more, each containing about 100,000 million stars. The Milky Way is one such galaxy, and our Sun one of its 100,000 million stars, while round it a few specks of planetary matter have been circulating for perhaps 5,000 million years or so; on one of them, because of the accidents of its climate, chemistry and temperature, at a given moment in time an already giant-sized molecule underwent a further mutation, thus becoming even larger and more complex than it was already, and in the process became the first living cell. Further random mutations chanced to occur – for as Professor Monod reminded us all in his book *Chance and Necessity* (1972), all is pure chance – and we are the end-products of that infinitesimally insignificant biochemical accident; and probably we are. But if that is all that can be said of us, then plainly to arrogate to ourselves any ideas of purpose, value or significance is absurd, as the atheist Existentialists, Jean-Paul Sartre and Albert Camus, with their literature and theatre of the absurd saw clearly enough, and as Monod emphasized when he wrote that man 'has emerged by chance. His duty, like his fate, is written nowhere ... Man as any other animal species is a pure accident of evolution; it might just as well not have appeared.' Thus Macbeth got it right when in terminal despair he cried out,

> To-morrow, and to-morrow, and to-morrow,
> Creeps in this petty pace from day to day,
> To the last syllable of recorded time;
> And all our yesterdays have lighted fools
> The way to dusty death. Out, out, brief candle!

Life's but a walking shadow, a poor player,
That struts and frets his hour upon the stage,
And then is heard no more; it is a tale
Told by an idiot, full of sound and fury,
Signifying nothing.

But while this may be acceptable as an intellectual hypothesis, no one lives as though it were true; we behave as though Macbeth was talking nonsense. Indeed, the play is a tragedy precisely because we see his outbreak of nihilism against the inexorable working out of God's law of justice, bringing in its wake divine retribution for the crimes he has committed; if life was really a 'tale told by an idiot', then Macbeth's crimes and those of his wife would not be crimes at all but mere incidents in the farce of living, and the murder of Duncan of no greater consequence than the swatting of a fruit fly. But, once again, no one lives as though this were true. For example, a casual acquaintance of mine had an experience during the Second World War which illustrates the point I am trying to make. I met him only once, but discovered that we shared much; we had both suffered the same kind of middle-class education, and like me he had rejected belief in God; growing up between the wars, we had both loathed the idea of war, subscribed to the usual liberal political ideals, which were virtually compulsory for anyone wishing to lay claim to a grain of intelligence at that time, and loved the arts. The major difference between us was that he was a German and, by the time I met him, a Lutheran pastor. I was unable to understand how anyone as cultured, charming and intelligent as he undoubtedly was could possibly have done anything as patently dotty as to become a Christian, let alone a clergyman, and I asked him how it had come about.

When the war had broken out he had been forced by events to join the Wehrmacht, much as I had joined the army here at home, and like me he had eventually been commissioned. He was posted to the Russian front, where after a time he had been given a job on the staff, and in 1943 or early 1944, when the Russians were advancing and the Germans being driven back, he was told to go from A to B on an errand; I have no idea what it was. At midday he found himself some miles west of the Russian town of Kiev, where a battle was raging, the thunder of the guns rumbling away over the eastern horizon, and there he decided to stop and eat a picnic lunch. He drove his car off the road – a long straight ribbon of road stretching away under a grey sky – and began to eat his sandwiches; as he did so, he noticed a small column of sorry and bedraggled-looking people approaching him from the east accompanied by a small guard of SS men armed with sub-machine guns. He did not pay much attention to them, and only later discovered that they were Jews being taken westwards to an extermination camp before the advancing Russians could reach them. One young woman had fallen fifty yards or so behind the main body, and she had done so because she was exhausted; her exhaustion was understandable, for she was in the last stages of pregnancy and she was carrying an infant in her arms and dragging a child of about eight by the hand as best she could despite the obvious exhaustion of the child. My acquaintance noticed one of the guards waiting behind to encourage her to keep up with the rest, and was horrified to observe that the way he did so was to knock her over the back of the neck with the butt of his sub-machine gun, while shouting oaths at her. The young woman fell face down on the road and began to vomit; when it became evident that despite a barrage of kicks to the stomach she would be unable to get up, the man shot her with a short and economical burst of fire, and left her corpse on the road with the two children screaming and scrambling over it.

My acquaintance was brought up against an immediate conviction, over which he could no more argue than he could argue about the fact that he breathed, that whatever else might be said about what he had just witnessed, it could not be adequately described in terms of the mere elimination of a chance biochemical accident of the earth's random physics and nothing more. Somehow he had to make sense of his primary human awareness of the horror of that incident and the value of the dead woman. His atheism made no sense of either except in terms of sociological conditioning and convenience, and he realized that, if the woman had no ultimate value, to be human is to be absurd; for the essence of being human, as opposed to being, say, a crocodile, a farmyard duck or a liver fluke, is to make value judgements. So he had to sit down and rethink his whole understanding of life; and after a time and some reluctance he came to the conclusion that only if there was some sort of truth in the symbolic statement that 'God so loved the world', could the value of that dead Jewess be established with any kind of sense or certainty, because then she could be seen to be valuable to the ground of all value and loved by the source of all love. It could, of course, be argued, as indeed it is by some sociologists and anthropologists, that value judgements are products of social factors, which is why they vary from society to society. Up to a point this is true, but only up to a point; for if that is all there is to be said of such judgements, and if there is no ultimate criterion by which they themselves may be valued, then it must be acknowledged that they are the products of majority opinion in any given society and no more. Thus, presumably, it was 'right' in Aztec Mexico to sacrifice 20,000 victims to the gods in a single day by opening their chests with an obsidian knife and ripping out their hearts, still beating and hot with blood; right, too, to practise female circumcision in various African countries, and to exterminate the Jews in Nazi Germany. My German acquaintance, however, concluded that if he was the only man in the world to condemn the murder of that Jewess on the road to Kiev as 'most foul, strange, and unnatural', he would be right and the other three thousand million inhabitants of the planet would be wrong. Somewhere along the line I came to the same conclusion; and I am persuaded, too, that most of my atheist friends would do so too, if put to it. For often their theory does not marry very well with their practice, which is frequently profoundly loving, moral and self-sacrificial, where the practice of Christians is sometimes at variance with their beliefs in the opposite direction.

I could have illustrated the point I have tried to make in that story of the young woman's murder on the road to Kiev less dramatically by recalling how I sat with my mother as she died a natural death in her eighties in a nursing home on Putney Hill after a stroke; for, once again, I could hardly have said, as she actually died, 'Right! So that's that! Another biochemical accident of the earth's chancy physics on its totally insignificant way towards a further chemical change. What's on the telly tonight?' Or I could have asked the reader whether he or she could have treated the first person they ever loved and held in their arms in all their naked vulnerability, surrender and uniqueness as no more than a biochemical accident. But I chose to give prominence to the story of the murder on the road to Kiev, partly because it deeply impressed me, and partly because the Christian faith is centred upon another story of a Jew unjustly murdered, this time on a hill near Jerusalem, and it therefore seemed particularly relevant to the subject of this book.

I realize, however, that this is to treat certain human emotions with a seriousness usually reserved for rational thinking on the ground that it is the intellect alone which leads to knowledge, while human emotions merely mislead or distract. But do they? No amount of rational thinking will do much to open my eyes to the splendour of Duccio's *Maesta* in Siena or my ears to the glory of Byrd's Five-part Mass, nor will rational thinking teach me as much about my lover, child, or lifelong friend as I will learn from loving them. Love is blind, it has been said, and if it is equated with infatuation it is indeed as blind as a bat; but with greater perception it has also been said that love and love alone sees and accepts a person whole and loves what it sees – virtues, faults and all. Only with someone we love do we dare walk naked and unashamed as we really are with all our physical blemishes unhidden: little pot belly, breasts beginning to resemble spaniel's ears rather than apples or pomegranates, appendix scar and varicose veins; and only to those who love us do we dare also to show our laziness, cowardice, kinkiness, vanity or what-have-you with no attempt to hide them. In the company of those whom we do not love, we don social masks with our clothes, thankfully hiding the truth about ourselves from prying eyes. Some of our emotions should therefore be treated with greater respect than it is currently fashionable to pay them, for they can reveal certain truths as nothing else can, and I make no apology for taking them seriously. They are part of our total experience and not to be despised.

Moreover, I am not at all sure that contemporary scepticism about value judgements in general and the value of a human being in particular is based as solidly on rational foundations as is often supposed. For foremost amongst contemporary objections to the idea of human beings having any ultimate value either as children of God or as supreme in the universe because of our god-like ability to take charge of our own destiny, is the perspective of modern cosmology; for when we consider the heavens, the sun and the moon and the stars revealed by twentieth-century astronomers, we too wonder what we can say of ourselves: we too ponder the question, What is man? 'If you wish to reflect upon our significance in the cosmos,' said Sir Bernard Lovell in his presidential address to the British Association for the Advancement of Science in 1975, 'it may be salutary to look towards the constellation of Coma, hold a penny at arm's length, and remember that you obscure from your vision a cluster of a thousand galaxies, 350 million light years away, and receding from us with a velocity of nearly 5,000 miles per second.' It is little consolation to recall that probably he was referring to an old-fashioned penny before the days of decimalization. We are so infinitely small and ephemeral in the perspectives of the galaxies and the quasars that it is understandable that we should feel ashamed of claims made in the past for our immortal significance and centrality; but this is precisely the kind of emotional reaction which we should indeed distrust. For what has size to do with value?

Undeniably, a human being is exceedingly small when measured on an astronomical scale (and almost unimaginably large against a sub-atomic ruler), but if you compare a human or any other living creature with a few light years of empty space, or with one of the spheres of nuclear heated gas which we call stars, or with a ball of dead rock like the Moon or Mars, which is the most significant, remarkable and rare? And since significance and rarity are characteristics of those things which we deem to be valuable, which is the most valuable? Even if you take only one part of a human being, an eye or that complex chemical sorting house, a liver, let alone a human brain, the same thing applies; they are astonishingly rare and sophisticated objects. For instance, in a popular book, *The Dragons of Eden* (1978), on the evolution of human intelligence, Dr Carl Sagan, Professor of Astronomy in Cornell University, pointed out that

> the human brain (apart from the cerebellum, which does not seem to be involved in cognitive functions) contains about ten billion switching elements called neurons . . . An average neuron in a human brain has between 1,000 and 10,000 synapses or links with adjacent neurons . . . If each synapse responds by a single yes-or-no answer to an elementary question, as is true of the switching elements in electronic computers, the maximum number of yes/no answers or bits of information that the brain could contain is $10^{10} \times 10^3 = 10^{13}$ . . . This is an unimaginably large number, far greater, for example, than the total number of elementary particles (electrons and protons) in the entire universe.

But if the human brain is, if not necessarily unique, certainly a rare and wonderful phenomenon to come across in the chilly and silent perspectives of cosmic immensity, how much more so is a whole human being, a laughing child, a dreaming lover, a dying Christ?

Since the time when I was confronted by the problem of the destiny and value of man, there has been another development in scientific cosmology which I find interesting, for it goes some way to replacing man at the centre of things as the flower of the whole cosmic evolutionary process rather than a mere accidental by-product of it. As a result of the Big Bang, we are now told, there might have been a number of different universes. As Dr Peacocke of Cambridge has pointed out in his book *Creation and the World of Science* (1979), if the proton–proton interaction had been slightly different at the time of the beginning of the expansion, then all the protons in the universe, which were the raw material of the heavier atoms in the stars, would have turned into the more inert helium in the early stages of the formation of a radically different universe from that which we know. To quote Bernard Lovell again, 'No galaxies, no stars, no life would have emerged. It would have been a universe unknowable by living creatures. The existence of a remarkable and intimate relationship between man, the fundamental constants of nature and the initial moments of space and time, seems to be an inescapable condition of our presence here.' B. Carter, quoted by Dr Peacocke, has gone further in an essay on 'Large Number Coincidences and the Anthropic Principle in Cosmology', which was published in a collection of essays entitled, *Confrontation of Cosmological Theories with Observational Data* (1974). He has argued that we live in what he has called an 'anthropic universe', contending that 'the Universe (and hence the fundamental parameters on which it depends) must be such as to admit the creation of observers within it at some stage.' What he seems to be saying is that our particular universe, out of an ensemble (his word) of possible universes, is a cognizable universe (his words again), which thus had to produce objects, creatures, able to observe and attempt to understand it at some point in its evolution; for this, indeed, it was made. How widely accepted this idea of an anthropic universe is amongst scientists, I do not know; but whatever else it may or may not do, it draws attention to the astonishing fact that, whether by a series of accidents or by design, 'in man, the stuff of the universe has become cognizing and self-cognizing', as Dr Peacocke has put it; 'far from man's presence in the universe being a curious and inexplicable surd, we find that we are remarkably and intimately related to it on the basis of this contemporary scientific evidence, which is indicative of a far greater degree of man's total involvement with the universe than ever before envisaged.'

However reliable this new hypothesis may be, it is so recent and I suspect so tentative that few people have heard of it. Instead, they still envisage themselves in the perspectives of Monod's vast and purposeless universe, in which the false equation of size with value, smallness with insignificance, has robbed many people both of the will to ask what their existence signifies and of the ability to judge its meaning or even to acknowledge that it has a meaning; for it has persuaded some people to believe that humanity's many attempts to discover that meaning, whether those attempts have been religious, artistic or philosophical, have been meaningless in themselves, because based on a meaningless question. But, once again, however much some people may deny that either humanity or they themselves have a meaning, it is something which everyone strives after, both corporately and individually, in one way or another, including, I suspect, those who deny the validity of such a search; they may even derive their own sense of significance from the fact that they are part of a chosen few, who are 'brave' and 'honest' enough to deny that such a search has any value or likelihood of success. For the fact is that, if psychiatry is to be trusted, the concept of meaning is something that few, if any, people can do without for long. Viktor Frankl in his book, *Psychotherapy and Existentialism*, went as far as to say in 1970 that most psychological malaise and distress suffered by people in our Western society can be attributed either to a suppressed or to an acknowledged conviction that their lives are meaningless. 'A psychiatrist today is confronted more and more with a new type of patient, a new class of neurosis, and a new sort of suffering, the most remarkable characteristic of which is the fact that it does not represent a disease in the proper sense of the term.' This is due, he goes on to say, 'to the experience of a total lack or loss of an ultimate meaning to one's existence that would make life worthwhile. The consequent void, the state of inner emptiness, is at present one of the major challenges to psychiatry.' Frankl describes how classical Freudian analysis explains human motivation in terms primarily of the search for pleasure and the will to survive, while Adlerian psychologists explain it primarily in terms of the will to power; but he gives it as his opinion that man 'is primarily motivated by the will to meaning ... What threatens contemporary man is the alleged meaninglessness of his life ... the existentialist vacuum within him.'

Of course there are other reasons for anxiety built into the human condition, death and guilt amongst them, and of these I shall have more to say later; but I cannot imagine that anyone is likely to disagree with Frankl when he says that anxiety over the suspicion that life may be totally meaningless is one of the worst fears that our flesh is heir to. Yet such a suspicion is as essentially human as the desire for love; all human beings know it at some time or other during their lives, whereas, as far as can be made out, other animals – giraffes, tapeworms, bed bugs – do not. Traditionally, the suspicion that life is futile and meaningless has been countered by belief in God or the gods; but such belief is no longer available to most people, and the result, as Frankl points out, is that many of them become neurotic. This makes the idea that religion itself is a form or result of neurosis difficult to accept. Of course, some neurotic people become religious, but if Frankl and others are right, it is not so much people who believe that their lives have some sort of religious or philosophical meaning who are neurotic but those who are convinced that they themselves and their existence are meaningless. But if the latter are right, and life is indeed without meaning, then the odd – almost paradoxical – conclusion must be accepted that the evolutionary process has shaped and formed human beings in such a way as to be in danger of becoming neurotic when not suffering from intellectual delusions of their own significance, and psychologically healthy only when labouring under a misapprehension: in other words, mentally sick when in possession of the truth, but happy, fulfilled and mentally healthy when grossly mistaken intellectually.

Of course, none of this proves that either God or the gods exist; there is no proof that we are not accidents of the earth's physics and that our gods are not figments of our imagination; and, of course, no proof that they are. But what it does make clear is that our decision as to whether God exists or not is not a decision in the realm of comfortable and largely irrelevant philosophical theory, but a decision about the nature and significance of ourselves. If there is a God, a human being is one kind of thing; if there is no God, he is another kind of thing altogether. Moreover, as Socrates saw, we need a raft on which to ride the seas of life, and the exigencies of living deprive us of the soft option of refusing to make a decision on the apparently plausible grounds that, since there is no conclusive evidence either way, the only sensible course is to keep an open mind on the matter. This sounds reasonable, but is in fact impossible; for an open mind, while it remains open, is a mind which has in practice rejected belief in God. I 'lie in' once a week on my day off, and while doing so I keep an open mind as to when I shall get out of bed and dress; and all the time my mind is open I am in bed. Furthermore, one of the exigencies, to which I have alluded, is the human need for some sort of hope based on personal meaning; if you deprive a person of all meaning, all self-understanding, hope withers and dies, and when that happens that person withers and dies soon afterwards.

Evidence that this is so was gathered by an Austrian Jew, Dr Bruno Bettelheim, who later became Professor of Psychology in the University of Chicago; it is set out in his book, *The Informed Heart* (1960), in which he describes his time in Dachau and Buchenwald during the last war. A pupil of Freud and a professional psychiatrist, he used his time in the concentration camps to study the effects of extreme adversity in general and the denial of meaning in particular upon his fellow inmates. Those whose self-understanding and esteem were bound up with their position in the family, their professional achievements and their social status, when confined in the camps and thus removed from everything which had hitherto given point to their lives, deteriorated with extraordinary speed. 'Their behaviour,' Bettelheim noted,

showed how little the apolitical German middle class was able to hold its own against National Socialism. No consistent philosophy, either moral, political, or social, protected their integrity or gave them strength for an inner

stand against Nazism. They had little or no resources to
fall back on when subject to the shock of imprisonment . . .
Prisoners who came to believe the repeated statements of
the guards that there was no hope for them, that they
would never leave the camp except as a corpse – who came
to believe that their environment was one over which they
could exercise no influence whatsoever – these prisoners
were, in a sense, walking corpses. In the camps they were
called 'Moslems' (*Muselmänner*) because of what was
erroneously viewed as a fatalistic surrender to the
environment, as Mohammedans are supposed to blindly
accept their fate. But these people had not, like real
Mohammedans, made an act of decision and submitted to
fate out of free will. On the contrary, they were people who
were so deprived of affect, self-esteem, and every form of
stimulation, so totally exhausted, both physically and
emotionally, that they had given their environment total
power over them . . . The deterioration of Moslems . . .
began when they stopped acting on their own; and that
was the moment when other prisoners recognized what
was happening and separated themselves from these
'marked' men, because any further association with them
could only lead to one's own destruction. At this point
such men still obeyed orders, but only blindly or automatically, no longer selectively or with inner reservation
or any hatred at being so abused. They still looked about,
or at least moved their eyes around. The looking stopped
much later, though even then they still moved their bodies
when ordered, but never did anything on their own any
more. Typically, this stopping of action began when they
no longer lifted their legs as they walked, but only shuffled
them. When finally even the looking about on their own
stopped, they soon died.

In contrast to these unfortunate people, those whose
inner integrity survived the camps best were those
whose hopes were of two kinds, personal and trans-

personal. Everyone's life is buoyed up by personal hopes:
hopes of passing an examination, of marrying a particular person, of becoming manager of the bank or the
Co-op or what-have-you, or just of going to Majorca
next year for a holiday; and of course these were the
hopes which died most quickly in the concentration
camps. But some people's lives were sustained, too, by
hopes pinned to something which transcended them as
individuals; the Communists believed that whatever
might happen to them personally, the ultimate victory
of the proletariat and the coming of the classless society
could not be defeated by Hitler or anyone else, and in a
sense that coming victory was vicariously their victory
too, even if they died in the camps before it could be
achieved. The Jehovah's Witnesses were buoyed up by
their own brand of faith, and so were many Christians,
who knew that, even if they themselves died in the
camps, the ultimate triumph of the kingdom of God was
assured. Dietrich Bonhoeffer was typical of many
others when, in a Nazi prison, he wrote, 'I believe that
God can and intends to let good spring from everything,
even from what is most evil. For this he needs human
beings who know how to turn all things to good.' In
similar vein, the sixty-eight-year-old Carthusian monk,
Bernard Lichtenberg, Dean of the Cathedral of St
Hedwig in Berlin, who was arrested for openly
encouraging his fellow Christians to help the Jews
against their Nazi persecutors, said in the last letter he
was to write before his death in 1943, 'I consider everything that happens to me, joyful or painful things,
elevating or depressing, in the light of eternity ... I
have enough courage to live for another twenty years,
but should I die today, may God's will be done.' And I
could give many more examples.

Plainly, the fact that many of those people whose lives

were filled with transpersonal hopes, notably the convinced Communists and Christians, did not dis-
integrate in the concentration camps as quickly as some
of those whose only hopes were bound up with their
own small ambitions and personal affairs, proves
nothing about either God or Karl Marx, but it does go to
show that hope and meaning are as necessary to human
fulfilment, perhaps even to human survival, as bread,
air and water. 'Where there is no vision, the people
perish' is a saying which has been put to the test again
and again in our own agnostic century, and has been
shown to be valid. So, once again, the question arises,
'Have we been evolved in such a way as to survive only
when sustained by delusions?' Whatever answer is given
to that question, it underlines the fact that the even
more fundamental question, 'God or no God?' is indeed
a question about our own nature and significance which
should not be swept under a carpet of indifference or
cynicism by anyone. And it is at this point that the
claims made by Christians for the man Jesus cannot be
ignored either; for if 'God was in Christ,' as St Paul put
it, God is one kind of God, while if Paul was talking
nonsense, the deity may be very different, and we
human beings will be different too.

VII

The Image of God

What does it mean to say that someone 'became a Christian'? The word 'Christian' is so loosely used that it can mean anything from a kind and loving sort of person who believes nothing to a bigoted fanatic who believes in the literal truth of the Bible, so that when Psalm 114 says that 'the hills skipped like young rams', it means that those same hills took off by the roots and bounded physically about the Sinai desert. Less extreme and more usual in ecclesiastical circles being 'a Christian' means that the person claiming to be a Christian at some point in his or her life 'accepted Jesus Christ as his or her personal Lord and Saviour'. That is a statement which itself needs defining but, however it may be defined, I certainly did not move from atheism to belief in God by way of any such sudden acceptance; for me the significance of Jesus came later, and for some people that admission will be taken as a proof that I did not become a Christian at all at that time. The order of events was different for me. As time passed and I ceased to mourn the death of my atheism, there came a point, as I have already said, not when I accepted Jesus as an intimate factor in my life but when I found that I believed that God existed. Comparing notes later with a friend who had become a Catholic after years of atheism, I said half in jest that I had believed in the Holy Ghost long before believing in either God the Father or Jesus Christ, whereupon she erupted in a spontaneous bubble of laughter and delighted agreement, for her own experience had been similar: a fact which greatly

irritated the atheist friend with whom we were staying at
the time, who thought us both totally mad. But
although my comment was a joke, to those who say that
no one can be a true Christian who has not consciously
come to belief through Christ I would suggest that this
may be to ignore the role of the Spirit.

However, if what happened to me at that time did not
make me a Christian, then it must have made me a
jubilant, if breathless and astonished, pagan; for once I
had got accustomed to the decision which I woke up one
morning to find planted in my head, namely that there
was a God – a decision which seemed to me to accord
with reason though also to transcend it – I found myself
filled with 'the type of thought' described by Professor
Jean-Pierre Vernant in his book, *Myth and Society in
Ancient Greece* (1980):

> The religion of the ancient Greeks and their pantheon of
> gods can be seen to be a system of classification, a particu-
> lar way of conceptualizing the universe, distinguishing
> between multiple types of force and power operating
> within it. So in this sense I would suggest that a pantheon,
> as an organized system implying definite relations
> between the various gods, is a kind of language, a particu-
> lar way of apprehending reality and expressing it in sym-
> bolic terms. I am even inclined to believe that in those
> ancient times there existed between language and religion
> a sort of co-naturality. When one considers religion as a
> type of thought, it appears to date back as far as language
> itself. What characterizes the human level as opposed to
> that of other creatures on the animal scale is the presence
> of these vast mediatory systems – language, tools and
> religion. However, man is not aware of having invented
> this language of religion. He feels that it is the world itself
> that speaks this language or, to be more precise, that
> *fundamental reality itself is a language. The universe appears
> to him as the expression of sacred powers which, in their own*

particular different forms, constitute the true texture of reality, the meaning that lies behind the symbols that manifest it. [The italics are mine.]

Apart from the fact that I should have classed the arts, rather than tools, or perhaps as well as tools, as one of man's 'vast mediatory systems', through which he apprehended reality in ancient times and indeed apprehends it today, that statement sums up better than I can do myself how I felt after I had given my atheism a decent burial and ceased to wear mourning clothes to mark its passing. The universe in which I found myself living was like a vast and miraculous work of art, shot through and through with transcendent order and harmony, and the world a place transparent to a mystery of being and creative power in which it seemed that 'the morning stars sang together, and all the sons of God shouted for joy'.

I am not convinced that all this necessarily made me a pagan rather than a Christian, for I am not convinced that Christian conversion must necessarily be as narrowly defined as some Christians would like; but if they are right, and I did in fact become a pagan at that time, I remain one, for the universe still has the same effect on me, and I am glad it does so. Statements like that in the celebrated hymn which speaks of 'the heathen in his blindness [who] bows down to wood and stone' seem to me to be proof of the writer's obtuseness, arrogance, and hopeless misunderstanding of the place of works of art in the practice of religion. Deutero-Isaiah was a great prophet, but he was a very bad art critic when he inveighed against the sculptor who chooses a bit of wood for a carving, 'Then it shall be for a man to burn, and he taketh thereof, and warmeth himself; yea, he kindleth it, and baketh bread; yea, he maketh a god and worshippeth it; he maketh a graven image, and falleth down thereto . . . and prayeth unto it, and saith, Deliver me, for thou art my God.' To be fair to Isaiah, he may have been so aware of the power of works of art to move the minds of men and women to contemplate the transcendent ideas they embody that he felt he had to mock them vigorously; but it is as absurd to suppose that the votaries of the gods he so much disliked actually *worshipped* the bits of wood or stone which represented them as to think that Orthodox Christians worship their icons. Orthodox Christians worship the powers embodied, expressed and represented in, through and beyond the images of them in their icons, and the 'heathen' of Isaiah's day doubtless did the same. Endowed with their own perception of reality, the pagans of the ancient world had a vision of the universe around them which I am glad to be able, in some measure, to share; and whatever some of their practices may have been, I do not believe that in essence their vision is incompatible with Christianity. Indeed, if Christ was the fulfilment of the old Jewish Law, I believe that there is a real sense in which he was also the fulfilment of the religions of the ancient world; memories of Attis, Adonis and Osiris inevitably stir in a literate mind when reading some parts of the New Testament, and this should not surprise or dismay anyone. On the contrary, it serves to underline the universality of Christ, and should be welcomed. Far from being incompatible with the pagan vision of the world at its best and most radiant, Christ made luminous sense of it: at least, he did so for me; for if the universe is like some transcendent work of art, the central claim made on behalf of the man Jesus is that he is the icon of God: that is to say, the image or physical object in, through, and beyond which men are challenged to see the transcendent God made present. By any definition, that makes him God's supreme work of art, the image which earthed divinity into humanity and the world, and gave the clue to the nature of the rest of his creation; and this, needless to say, I found immensely exciting and wholly acceptable.

But plainly it poses problems. It is one thing to believe in a God who/which is not merely another being, somewhat like ourselves only larger and super-natural, but rather the spiritual reality underlying all things, which is how God is defined in a recent book by Professor Keith Ward of King's College, London, him-self an ex-atheist – a definition of the indefinable that is as acceptable as any theological proposition is ever likely to be. But it is altogether another thing to go on to say that this infinite underlying spiritual reality somehow became a man at a particular time and place in history. How can the former concept of God be reconciled to the idea of God as a person? How can a statement by the man Jesus like, 'God is a spirit and those that worship him must worship him in spirit and in truth,' be married to such different commands as, 'When ye pray, say, Abba, father', especially when it is recalled that the word 'Abba' was the diminutive for 'father', rather like Papa? It is not a new problem. St Paul knew that the idea of an incarnate God, whom men could crucify, was 'foolishness to the Greeks and a stumbling block to the Jews': that is to say, idiocy to intellectuals and near-blasphemy to convinced monotheists; but the fact that it is an age-old problem, which exercised the best minds of the Greek world from St Paul's day right through the patristic age, is no excuse for not looking at it again on the grounds that it has been resolved once and for all in the great Christological formularies of the Church, or conversely on the grounds that it is such a deep mystery that it is useless to delve into it. It is indeed a mystery, and the participants in the great Christological debates of the early Church may well have plumbed it as deeply as anyone ever will; but they thought in different categories from those in which we and our contemporaries think, and the conclusions to which they came are almost wholly unintelligible today to all but a handful of theologians, and this is a far from satisfactory situation. For if the idea of an incarnate God was foolishness to the Greeks and a stumbling block to the Jews of St Paul's day, the apparently unintelligible statements in the Christian formularies and creeds which churchgoers are required to say can be very serious stumbling blocks to some of the most honest of them, to whom intellectual integrity is important, and baffling nonsense to many highly intelligent non-church-goers, who realize nevertheless how much they are missing by living without any religious faith. Therefore we must try to understand the problem all over again in terms which are less strange to our contemporaries if we wish them to take the claims made for Christ seriously. I feel very strongly that someone must have the courage to do this, for I know what it feels like to look with longing and yet with angry bafflement at the apparently hopeless unintelligibility of the Church's proclamation of its faith in Christ; and although I realize how rash I am to say any such thing, I believe that we may be in a better position to reassess the problem in the latter half of the twentieth century than our forefathers were.

For the problem is basically that of the relationship of an image to the reality imaged: that is to say, how can the particular historical man, Jesus of Nazareth, possibly relate to the spiritual reality underlying all things, which is what God must be if he/it exists at all? And we are the first generation of human beings to live in a world which knows through the work of the sub-atomic physicists that we perceive it and everything in it in images: the first generation to know for sure that what we hear, taste, see and touch are largely creations of our own minds, a rich tissue of images of the very different reality of the sub-atomic world of electrons and protons and the rest which constitute the physical reality underlying all things. It may seem an absurdly simplistic question, but if reality differs so much from our image of it in the realm of science and everyday experience, why should not the reality and image of God be as different in the realm of religious definition and experience? The fact is that images are the primary stuff of our apprehension; they are fundamental, both to our perception of the world and to the possibility of our understanding it. They are both the raw material upon which our intellects work analytically and the links which connect us to the underlying reality of the world; and this is true in science, the arts and religion. Moreover, the image is not to be despised as 'a mere image', as though it were inferior to the reality it images, nor written off as basically inessential to that reality; for, to borrow an analogy from the arts, it would be the height of folly to say, 'How marvellous Rembrandt's portrait of his son Titus is! What a painting! It is a profound statement of the loveliness, vulnerability and preciousness of the boy, but do burn the picture; it is quite inessential to the vision it embodies and expresses.' What Rembrandt had to say about his son is expressed and embodied in the material object of canvas and dried paint which constitutes the picture, and can no more be divorced from it than the sub-atomic reality of the paving stones upon which I walk can be divorced from the hard surface which saves me from falling head over heels when I go shopping. So that, even if God is eternally greater than his images, as Christians have always believed, and as

Christ himself repeatedly emphasized – 'The Father is greater than me', 'Why callest thou me good? None but God alone is good' – the fact that his image in Christ is apparently very different from his reality-in-himself should constitute no insuperable barrier to believing in Christ as the icon of God: that is to say, as the physical object in, through, and beyond which men are challenged to see the transcendent God made present. One could perhaps sum up the problem of understanding God by saying that, while the idea of God as the spiritual reality underlying all things is unimaginable but by no means unintelligible, Christ as the image of God is, in the nature of the thing, imaginable but difficult, if not impossible, adequately to define, analyse or understand intellectually. So, however, is the significance of a late Beethoven quartet. In both the mystery remains a mystery, and yet in both the mystery is revealed.

I suspect, however, that as far as images are concerned most people do not think first of Jesus as the image of God but as the son of God; it is the most powerful and on the surface the simplest of all the images applied to him. Indeed, I further suspect that many people do not think of the term 'son of God', as applied to Jesus, as an image at all but rather as a simple biological description of him: that is to say, they think of Jesus as the son of God in the same way as young Bill Smith is the son of his father, John Smith. Millions of people have thought of him in this way down the centuries without being bothered by doubts, and some accept the idea today with the same ease; but others do not. For them, once you proclaim that the image of Jesus as the 'son of God' is not an image but a biological fact, credulity is stretched to breaking point, and they feel forced to reject the Christian faith. Some people would argue that they should learn to accept it, as their forefathers did, or go without. But it is not as easy as that, for their forefathers in New Testament times had very different ideas about biological origination from those of today, and if you apply modern biological knowledge to the term 'son of God' you make theological nonsense of the doctrine of Christ. For if that term is to be understood in modern biological terms, then Jesus must have been half God and half man, a hybrid; and this has never been either Christian belief or Christian teaching, which proclaims him to be wholly God and wholly man: God made man. This is precisely what the earliest Christians would have understood by the term 'son of God', for the Jewish contemporaries of Jesus believed that the male semen, injected into the female during the course of copulation, actually grew into the child in the mother's womb, her only part in the whole affair being to provide the growing child with a tent of flesh in which this could happen. In other words, children originated in the creative organs of the father and were a result of the father's will and action alone. Thus the story of the virgin birth in St Luke's Gospel and in St Matthew's would have been taken to mean that the child Jesus was the result of an initiative taken by God and made possible by the passive role of Mary, the result being, not a cross physically between God and man, but God made flesh, God incarnate, true God made true man; or as St Paul put it, 'God was in Christ.'

Biologically, this may make little or no sense today; but in terms of image and reality it seems to me to make pellucid sense. For the statement that Jesus was 'the image of God' is not very different from Paul's statement to the Colossians that 'in him dwelleth all the fullness of the Godhead bodily'; and that in its turn is not so different from St Augustine's statement that '*Verbum*

... *ars quaedam omnipotens atque sapientis Dei*': 'the
Word ... is, in a way, the art of the almighty and wise
God'. The idea of Christ as God's supreme work of art,
his own self-portrait, was an analogy which explained
many things to me about Christ which otherwise eluded
my understanding altogether, and it excited me greatly.
'Art,' said Herbert Read in *Art and Society* (1937), 'is a
mode of expression, a language ... In all its essential
activities art is trying to tell us something'; and the
notion of Jesus as God's mode of self-expression, in and
through whom he was speaking and trying to tell people
something about himself, let alone doing something for
the world, lit up the gospel for me in a way that nothing
else had or, I suspect, could have done. Moreover, it
made sense of other aspects of it; for instance, one of the
things that seems to have worried the earliest Christians
was the fact that very few people noticed that 'God was
in Christ' during his lifetime. Why were his contemporaries so blind? In St Mark's Gospel it is said that they
were blinded by God, as Isaiah had prophesied that
they would be, 'That seeing they may see and not perceive, and hearing they may hear and not understand,
lest haply they should turn again, and it should be
forgiven them.' This implies that Jesus went around
purposely baffling his hearers, because God did not
want them to understand what he was saying to them;
but this paints such an extraordinary picture both of
God and of Jesus, trying to frustrate their own express
purposes of salvation, that it is difficult to accept. It
seems far more likely that Mark, or the man from whom
Mark gathered his information, plagued by the question
as to why people had been so blind to the true significance of Jesus, if he had indeed been the son of God, lit
upon a passage in Isaiah which seemed to solve the
problem: God had blinded them to the truth.

But there are simpler explanations of the blindness of Jesus's contemporaries. I do not want to push the analogy between Jesus and a work of art too far – and, of course, I know that it is no more than an analogy – but if there is any truth in it at all, then the blindness of his contemporaries is perhaps not very surprising; for the greater and more original a work of art and its imagery may be, just as the greater and more original a radically new idea in science may be, the more likely it is to be greeted at first with hostility and misunderstanding. 'Let those with ears to hear, hear', was a saying applied to the parables of Jesus, but it could have been addressed with equal pertinence to the contemporaries of Galileo as well as to the contemporaries of those legions of great artists and musicians down the ages whose works have been greeted with ridicule and blindness during their lifetime, only to be valued and understood after their creators' deaths.

But there is another and even simpler reason why the contemporaries of Jesus found it so difficult to see in him anything more than an ordinary man: he *was* an ordinary man. The Jews had very clear ideas about what the long-awaited Messiah would be like, when at last he came to usher in the kingdom of God and confound the enemies of his chosen people; and the last thing they expected was an ordinary man. They expected a supernatural being, all-powerful and intent upon vindicating his elect by divine force, while burning their Gentile oppressors like chaff, and Jesus did not fit that bill. It is a point well taken by Professor John Bowker, the Dean of Trinity College, Cambridge, in his book *The Religious Imagination and the Sense of God* (1978); speaking of St Paul's time he has pointed out that 'there were many prophets, many workers of miracles, many gods, many religions in the world in which Paul lived; there

were myths of dying and rising gods, mysteries which
opened, or claimed to open, a way through death. But
Jesus was open to prosaic observation. He was tangled
up in the human situation.' The human ordinariness of
Jesus is emphasized equally strongly in the New Testament itself, where the author of the Epistle to the Heb-
rews says that Jesus was 'in all things like unto his
brethren': that is to say, subject to death and indignity
and unequivocally human; and St John reminds his
readers that 'That which we have heard, that which we
have seen with our eyes, that which we have beheld, and
our hands have handled ... we declare to you.' This
human ordinariness of Jesus forms the background to
the story of Peter's confession of faith, when in reply to
Jesus's question, 'Who do you say that I am?' he said,
'Thou art the Christ', whereupon Jesus's immediate
response was 'Blessed art thou, Simon bar Jonah! Flesh
and blood hath not revealed this to thee, but my father
in heaven.' In addition to emphasizing the ordinariness
of Jesus, this story makes the further point that the truth
is revealed to Peter; it is not the result of his own human
achievement. Peter falls through Koestler's trap-door,
and is shown by God – the spiritual reality behind all
things – the underlying truth of Jesus the man. His eyes
are opened to the truth. It is a flash in the pan, however,
as his next remarks demonstrate, and it is only after he
and the other disciples have been shown the truth
behind the ordinary death of Jesus, namely that it is the
gate to life, that he ceases to be Simon bar Jonah and
becomes Peter the God-born rock.

But if the reason for Jesus's contemporaries' blindness to his true significance was due partly to their
understandable failure to penetrate the ordinariness of
his humanity and partly to the same sort of blindness as
has so often been shown by people throughout history to

works of art, it is perhaps worth noticing here that one of the characteristics of such works is precisely their apparent ordinariness; though perhaps simplicity might be a better description, for often it is this astonishing simplicity which differentiates great works of art from merely good ones. In the Louvre there is a picture by Simone Martini of Christ carrying his cross which illustrates the point I am trying to make, though I could have chosen hundreds of others to perform the same service; it is ten inches by four inches of painted board in more or less bright colours; the draughtsmanship is not much better or much worse than that of other early fourteenth-century works, the composition no more remarkable than that of similar paintings of the time, and yet it is almost literally a small miracle of grace and truth to those with eyes to see. A Rembrandt brush-drawing in the British Museum of a girl sleeping is almost more remarkable because it is monochrome and must have been done in less than five minutes; it makes you want to say, 'Anyone could have done that!' and in the same breath, 'What a miracle!'

In view of all this, it is perhaps not surprising that so few people who came face to face with Jesus in his lifetime were impressed, for he was too simple, too ordinary, for them; they were looking for the wrong kind of miracle and the wrong kind of Messiah. That this was so was made plain enough when Jesus chided them with the words, 'Unless ye see signs and wonders, ye will not believe . . . it is an evil and adulterous generation that seeketh after a sign.' But, of course, the contemporaries of Jesus were not the only people who have looked for signs and wonders of the wrong kind; every generation is liable to do so, not excluding our own, which runs after the leaders of ecstatic sects, divine healers, hypnotic Indian gurus and charismatic miracle workers in the suburbs of California and elsewhere. But precisely because Jesus was both an ordinary man and also the image of God, the place where Christians should seek the truth and vision of God is primarily in and through the ordinary; for the revelation of transcendent splendour in and through the ordinary is the heart of true miracle:

> . . . a world in a grain of sand,
> And heaven in a wild flower
> . . . infinity in the palm of your hand,
> And eternity in an hour.

It is a vision of your neighbour as an image of the mystery of God, and the great nebula in Andromeda as 'the work of thy fingers'; and Christ as both son of man and Icon of God.

Even if only some small part of this is true, it seems to me that there is no need to look much further for what unites art, science and religious faith; for the world's artists have always sought to see the underlying order, truth and harmony of things, and so have the scientists. It was when I reached this point in my fumbling search for a new set of ideas with which to furnish my head, left empty, dusty and uninhabited since I had thrown away its atheist fittings, that I began to realize that if the 'earth and common face of nature' had spoken rememberable things to Wordsworth, the ordinary man and common face of Christ were speaking even more rememberable things to me; and one of those things concerned me and my own nature. For if the Christian faith sees in Jesus the clue to the nature of God, it also sees in him the clue to the true nature of human beings as they can and should be. 'He came unto his own,' said St John in the prologue to his Gospel, 'and they that were his own

received him not. But as many as received him, to them
gave he power to become the sons of God'; and later in
his First Epistle, he goes further and says firmly,
'Beloved, now are we the sons of God ...' Paul said
much the same to the Christians in Rome, namely that
'as many as are led by the spirit of God, they are the sons
of God'; and he encouraged those in Philippi not to
bicker amongst themselves, 'That ye may be blameless
and harmless, the sons of God.' This central belief
about humanity's true destiny and nature did not
change, for a hundred years later Irenaeus, who was
bishop of Lyons in the middle of the second century,
insisted that God became man in order that men might
attain their true destiny and become sons of God.

This was a new kind of anthropology for me; wherever I looked at the Christian doctrine of man, I found
the same emphasis upon possibility, opportunity and
becoming, and it made sense. Human beings, it
seemed, were neutral things, potentially either demonic
or godlike, battle-grounds upon which conflicting
forces were at war, and the issue of the war was one of
life or death. Having watched the rise of Nazism in
Germany, during which the world witnessed something
very like the demon possession of one of the most civilized peoples on earth, I had no difficulty in accepting
that side of the Christian analysis of the human condition. It made sense, too, of my own nature and inner
conflicts. But above all, on the positive side, the doctrine of man as an image and child of God went a long
way to answering the question posed by my corpses. I
was no longer forced to betray my own deepest human
awareness by consigning that Jewish woman, murdered
on the road to Kiev, to the rubbish heap of time past as a
biological accident of a senseless universe. Meanwhile,
on the positive side, it made sense, too, of those whom I

loved and of the preciousness of people as images of a mystery greater than themselves, and sense finally of the artist's vision of the ordinary world as a monstrance of great splendour. In fact, things began to hang together in a web of meaning and mystery, sense and disclosure, art and faith, and although I was still very frightened by the thought of becoming a Christian, I knew that I was being carried along on a tide of ideas and perception which I was quite unable to control or resist; and God alone knew where it was taking me.

VIII

The Birth of the Images

It will have occurred to many people already that it is all very well to say that Jesus was an ordinary man, 'in all things like unto his brethren', but if he was no more than that, why on earth did anyone ever come to believe that he was also the image of God? No one has ever attracted such a burgeoning of images as Jesus, the Jewish boy from Nazareth. He has been called the image of God, true vine, tree of life, branch of righteousness, well of living water, rose of Sharon, good shepherd, root of David, sun of righteousness, new Adam, bishop of our souls, rock of ages, mighty God, consolation of Israel, king, morning star, desire of all nations, bundle of myrrh, lion of the tribe of Judah, bread of life, corner-stone, lamb of God, Immanuel, horn of salvation, wisdom of God, tabernacle, day-star, first-born of the dead, brightness of the Father's glory, Son of God, and so many other things that Alexander Cruden, compiling his Concordance to the Bible in the first half of the eighteenth century, listed two hundred names and images which have been applied to him. They were not applied to Joseph his father, James his brother, Peter or John, but to Jesus alone, and the question again is, Why?

Images are the stock-in-trade of artists and poets. They resort to them because ordinary words are unable to bring out the full significance of whatever the artist or poet is concerned with. The words used in everyday speech and common prose are designed to describe a thing or event with the minimum fuss and the maxi-

mum objectivity; artists and poets are concerned to
evoke an understanding of that thing or event, casting
the mind of the spectator or the reader beyond the mere
thing or event to an awareness of its value, splendour,
horror, beauty or terror. Thus the phrase, 'Cry
"Havoc!" and let slip the dogs of war', is far more
evocative of Mark Antony's anger, the evil of Caesar's
unavenged murder and the horror of the war that it is
about to provoke than such a phrase as, 'Hostilities will
commence at 0900 hours.' Plainly, then, the images
which clustered round the figure of Jesus were meant to
bring out his significance in a manner beyond the capability of straight, everyday prose. Thus Mark, the
author of the earliest Gospel, began with an immensely
powerful and evocative image: 'The beginning of the
Gospel of Jesus Christ, the Son of God', he wrote, where
an entry in *Who's Who* would doubtless have run, 'Jesus,
s. of Joseph and Mary, b. 25 Dec. AD 1; educ. Nazareth
Synagogue; baptized, Jordan, *circa* AD 28 . . .' etc., etc.
This use of poetry and art by the writers of the New
Testament has far-reaching consequences which are all
too easily forgotten, the chief of which is that all our
principal sources of information about the life and death
and teaching of Jesus are much more closely akin to
works of art than to manuals of statistics, parish regis-
ters or collections of bare historical facts. The various
books in the New Testament are like paintings by
different artists of the same subject seen from slightly
different points of view; they vary in colour, interpretation and emphasis as, say, a series of landscapes by
Cézanne, Van Gogh, Gauguin, Seurat and Sisley of
Mont Ste Victoire in Provence would have varied, had
all those men been set to paint it. None of them would
have been primarily interested in making a detailed or
accurate record of exactly what they saw, leaf by leaf,

rock by rock, field by field, and passing cloud by passing cloud, though each of their paintings would have been recognizably of the same physical mountain; even so, their works would have been of little use to geologists, botanists or agriculturalists of a later time, who might have wanted to gather information about that part of Provence in the late nineteenth century. Instead, they would have interested only those people of all ages who found in them glimpses of the splendour and harmony of what Cézanne called 'the spectacle that Pater Omnipotens Aeterne Deus spreads out before our eyes'; but to people so interested the paintings would have been far from valueless or uninteresting; for, vastly to over-simplify, where Cézanne would have said something about the structure of the landscape (and not only of *the* landscape, but of landscape in general) and Van Gogh something about its sun-drenched vitality, Seurat and the others would have added their own distinctive contributions to an 'understanding' of the massive and transcendent splendour of Mont Ste Victoire and of the world of which it is a part. As a result, the observers of their various works would have gone away enriched: more enriched than they would have been by any one painting alone, but still no better informed than before about the height of the mountain, the composition of its rocks or the fertility of its soil. They would have been given a vision of the mountain and the world, not a factual account of it, though the vision would have been impossible had there been no mountain there in actual, hard fact in the first place; indeed, they would have been given a number of visions, and each of them would have been in the nature of a challenge to the spectators to say, 'Is Mont Ste Victoire – indeed, is the world – this kind of place, or isn't it?'

Perhaps I have pushed the analogy too far, though I

hope not. Be that as it may, I still have not answered the question as to why it was round the man Jesus that this wealth of imagery accrued and why it was of him that Matthew, Mark, Luke, John, Paul and the rest painted their visionary portraits – their landscapes of his life and death – if that is a permissible way of describing the New Testament books. The clue may be found, I think, in the story, recounted by two of the Evangelists, of the reaction of the people of his own home town to him, when he returned there during the course of his ministry; convinced of his ordinariness, they turned to each other in astonishment, saying, 'Is not this the carpenter's son? Is not his mother called Mary? and his brethren, James, and Joseph, and Simon, and Judas? And his sisters, are not they all with us?' But they made the cause of their astonishment plain when they added, 'Whence then hath this man this wisdom and these mighty works?' That is the point. His contemporaries were convinced of his ordinary humanity; there was no doubt in their minds about that, but at the same time they were baffled by a suspicion that somehow God was acting and speaking through him; or if God was not doing so, then something very like God was at work in him: a demon perhaps, some people concluded. In John's portrait, Jesus himself is made to claim that it was indeed God who was speaking and acting through him. 'As my father hath taught me, I speak these things . . . the works that I do in my father's name bear witness of me.' Later, he is even more explicit, saying to his disciples, 'He that hath seen me hath seen the father . . . I am in the father, and the father in me. The words that I say unto you I speak not from myself; but the father abiding in me doeth his works. Believe me that I am in the father, and the father in me; or else believe me for the very works sake.' Whether Jesus himself spoke these actual words is a matter of dispute amongst biblical scholars, but in this context it does not greatly matter, for they certainly sum up what people came to believe of him, namely that God was speaking and acting through him; and that is a very remarkable thing to believe of anyone. Plainly, something must have happened to make them do so. So, once again, the question is, What happened?

In one sense the answer is obvious enough, for in all the Gospels there are miracle stories which challenge the reader to answer the question, 'What manner of man is this?', and of course they are intended to pose just such a question. But did the miracles happen? As parables, the miracle stories make great sense. The story of the healing of a man born blind, which is told in John's Gospel, is a case in point; to some people who refused to believe that Jesus could have given him his sight, he protested, 'One thing I know, that whereas I was born blind, now I see'; and I know just how he felt. For years I, too, had been blind to many things which later in life I began to see clearly for the first time after God had opened my eyes to what I had been missing. Similarly, the stories of Jesus raising the dead to new life made sense of my own experience of being given a new life in a new sort of world with new perspectives and new horizons. But these stories are presented by the Evangelists as facts, not parables, and inevitably this creates a problem for most twentieth-century readers, who are prejudiced against the idea that such miraculous happenings are possible, though others, who have had experiences of a radical change of mind from unbelief to belief similar to my own, seem to find no difficulty in accepting the miracle stories *au pied de la lettre*.

However, things are not as simple as that; in some ways I wish they were, and perhaps those who find no difficulty in believing in the literal truth of the miracle stories are the lucky ones, going straight to the religious truth contained in them like homing pigeons. But this is not possible for everyone, and it is not only twentieth-century prejudice which makes some of the miracle stories difficult to accept at their face value; the real difficulty is created by the New Testament itself, which contains other stories which are very hard, if not impossible, to reconcile with the idea that Jesus went around during his ministry raising the dead and performing a number of sensational miracles which could have left no doubt in anyone's mind that he was what the Church later claimed him to have been, namely the miracle-working son of God. Again and again, the Evangelists report him as refusing to give people incontrovertible signs, miraculous proofs that it was indeed God who was at work in and through him. It was, he said, 'an evil and adulterous generation' that sought such things, and he flatly refused to provide them. Indeed, right at the beginning of his ministry, one of the temptations to which he had been subjected in the wilderness had been to dazzle people by casting himself down from the pinnacle of the temple in order to be rescued in spectacular fashion by a posse of angels so that the world could do nothing but hail him as the miraculous son of God; and this, too, he had firmly rejected. The Superman syndrome was not for him.

How, then, can these two apparently irreconcilable aspects of the Gospels be reconciled, and how can the stories of Jesus's refusal to work miracles be understood alongside such stories as that of the raising of Lazarus? The Gospels are more like works of art than factual records, and the purpose of a work of art is to 'bring out the significance, transcendent value or beauty of its principal subject. There is no doubt at all that this was the purpose of the authors of the New Testament books, their subject being Jesus, and his significance for them being God-made-present and active; and there are indications that some of the miracle stories may have started life during the period of oral tradition, when the stories about Jesus and his actions were passed by word of mouth, in rather different forms, and have been adapted to serve that purpose. For instance, both Matthew and Mark report that, on encountering a fruitless fig tree Jesus, who was hungry at the time, cursed it, and it promptly withered and died. Apart from the fact that such an irrational action on Jesus's part would have been out of character, Luke tells substantially the same story as a parable: that is to say, a barren fig is good for nothing but to be destroyed, the moral being that if Israel ceases to bear the fruit of righteousness desired by God, it deserves no better fate than that of the barren fig. It seems highly probable, therefore, that the versions of this story in Matthew and Mark are dramatically enhanced versions of Luke's parable, in which over the years, with the most laudable of intentions, the words 'Jesus said . . .' have been transformed by the tellers of the story into 'Jesus did . . .'

But there is another aspect of the miracle stories which is easily overlooked, namely that many of them are not about actions which we should necessarily class as miraculous at all. I personally believe that God heals people primarily through the skill, knowledge and labours of the medical profession, but doctors themselves would, I think, be the first nowadays to admit that many human ills are psychosomatic in origin and nature, and thus open to cure by suggestion and various means other than those normally used by medical practitioners, though they themselves often prescribe placebos with salutary effect. There is, therefore, no reason to doubt that some of the stories about Jesus forgiving people's sins, healing their diseases and casting out their demons are rooted and grounded in historical fact. We should probably have classed some of his 'patients' as schizophrenics, hysterics or neurotics, but to the contemporaries of Jesus, who believed that disease was the result of sin and that only God could forgive sin, their cures would have been manifest pointers to the fact that God was at work in and through this extraordinary, and yet at the same time this entirely ordinary, man in their midst; and the report of such actions would have been enough to start rumours circulating that 'a great prophet is arisen among us, and God hath visited his people'.

But although this may be true, it does not solve the problem of the birth of the images. Indeed, it seems certain that during Jesus's lifetime people did not get much beyond the point of suspecting that either God or a demon was at work in him. Even the disciples did not realize the truth until after his death, and as far as the majority of his contemporaries were concerned he puzzled rather than convinced them. So why did the writers of the New Testament, the painters of his portraits, unanimously present him to their readers as someone through whom, to their certain knowledge, God had acted with almost literally earth-shaking power? The answer, of course, is to be found in the events of Easter; it was not until after Easter that they began to acclaim him as the Christ, and everything written both by St Paul and the Evangelists was written in the light of that acclamation: that is to say, in the light of the conviction that God had raised Jesus from the dead on Easter morning and 'made him Lord and Christ'. Everything started there.

If the other miracle stories represent a post-Easter

conviction that God had been at work in Jesus, the resurrection is presented as the supreme act of God wrought through him, a vindication of all that he had said and done, and thus the greatest of all reasons for faith in God and in Jesus; it was the supreme 'sign' of the power and faithfulness of God. However God-forsaken a place the world might seem to be from time to time in all its darkness, violence and death, and however many men and women down the ages might cry like Jesus in an extremity of desolation, 'My God, my God! Why hast thou forsaken me?', God was not dead or deaf on Good Friday, and by raising Jesus from the dead on Easter Day, creating life and light out of the bloody destruction and darkness of Calvary, he demonstrated once and for all his concern for this world and all those who live and die in it. He does not save us from disaster, as we should like; he saves us beyond disaster. At least, that is the gospel, the 'good news' which intoxicated the earliest Christians, so that John could assure his readers that 'God so loved the world that he gave his only-begotten Son, to the end that all that believe in him should not perish but have everlasting life.' Thus the resurrection was and is the heart of Christian faith, as a chorus of contemporary theologians are prepared to affirm. 'For them [the first disciples] the gospel without the resurrection was not merely a gospel without its final chapter; it was not a gospel at all,' wrote Michael Ramsey, one-time Archbishop of Canterbury, and he was echoed by Professor Günther Bornkamm of Heidelberg University, who said that 'there could be no gospel, not one account, no letter in the New Testament, no faith, no Church, no worship, no prayer in Christendom to this day without the message of the resurrection.'

*   *   *

I had read none of these learned works at the time, but I
had read the Gospels, and the fact that the Christian
faith was born at Easter was obvious enough; Paul had
told the Christians in Corinth that 'if Christ hath not
been raised, your faith is vain.' Thus, the resurrection is
the crunch-point of the gospel – the *sine qua non* of the
Christian faith; and yet paradoxically no one saw it. It
took place – if, indeed, it took place at all – in the
darkness of a rock-cut Herodian tomb, where the spirit
of God brooded over the corpse of a dead man in a new
genesis, a new act of creation; the birth of the church
and its explosive faith were the results of that hidden
encounter, that germinal event. In a further paradox,
although this is the heart of the gospel, to ask the
Gospels to explain exactly what that event was – to
demand to know just what happened – is to demand the
impossible. It is a bit like asking one of those hypotheti-
cal paintings of Mont Ste Victoire to reveal the geologi-
cal secrets of the mountain: how was it formed in the
first place, and is it composed of igneous, sedimentary
or volcanic rock? The paintings are not patient of such
material questions, though they are capable of assuring
the beholder that Mont Ste Victoire is *there*, and that the
painters were confronted with a real mountain in all its
solidity and splendour. The analogy is not exact, but in
a somewhat similar way the Gospels are not patient of
the kind of material questions about the resurrection
which we should dearly like to put to them: was the
corpse of Jesus resuscitated without being changed or
was it transformed in some way, or did the disciples
meet a spiritually recreated Jesus? But if the Gospels
cannot answer these questions they can assure us, I
believe, that the events described by the disciples, the
early Church and the writers of the New Testament
were real enough; they did not sit down and write about

a non-event but about a very real *sainte victoire*. Like the mountain, it was *there*.

So what facts do the various accounts of the resurrection contain? They contain a record of fear, bewilderment and failure on the part of the disciples as the end of Jesus's ministry and life drew near. After years of being unsure of what to make of him – years of oscillation between hope and depression – when he was arrested by the Jewish authorities, they deserted him; understandably terrified, they left him to die alone, while Peter disclaimed any knowledge of him to save his own skin. Their disillusionment was completed by his execution as a common criminal, and after his death and hasty burial, dismayed and appalled by what had happened, they hid themselves behind closed doors for fear of sharing his fate. Since this account of their behaviour could scarcely reflect more shamefully upon the disciples, we may be as sure as we can be about anything that it happened; historians do not invent shameful stories about their heroes, and since Peter and the other disciples were the heroes of the early Church, its founding fathers, there is every reason to believe that they behaved in this way at the time of the crucifixion.

What is equally sure, as sure as the Battle of Waterloo, is that after the crucifixion and death of Jesus they were quite suddenly transformed into a bunch of men who were so completely convinced that the world had failed to destroy him on Calvary, and that God had given him the victory by raising him from the dead, that nothing – not even the threat of martyrdom or even actual martyrdom – could thereafter persuade them that they were mistaken. This man, whom the world had killed ignominiously and with the utmost brutality as a criminal agitator and a failed prophet, they proclaimed to be the son of God; this man, who died alone, nailed helplessly to a cross, unable to move hand or foot and covered all over with blood and sweat and the spittle of a jeering crowd, they proclaimed to be victor over death; this man, who by any normal standards had plumbed the depths of human weakness and dereliction, they proclaimed to be the wielder of all power in heaven and on earth; this man, who had been buried in a rock-cut tomb over the door of which had been rolled a large stone like a mill-stone weighing half a ton or more, they proclaimed to be alive; they had met him and spoken to him. Their fears and doubts disappeared on Easter morning like mist before the heat of the rising sun and, like any other historical phenomenon, this transformation of the disciples, this birth of faith out of the womb of despair, must have been caused by something. As everyone knows, they themselves said that it was the result of discovering his tomb to be empty and subsequently meeting the risen Christ, and those who wish to deny that the resurrection ever happened must provide some alternative explanation of this radical change of heart and mind in the disciples. This has always been recognized, and three alternative hypotheses have been put forward by various people in the past.

The first and simplest suggestion is that Jesus survived the crucifixion and that the disciples met him on Easter morning while under the impression that he had died on Friday; but this does not stand much examination. A good deal is known about the manner in which the Romans executed condemned men, and the chances of anyone surviving the treatment reserved for them were remote in the extreme. As in Jesus's case, condemned men were first subjected to a flagellation with a five-thonged leather whip, a *flagellum*, with pieces of metal tied into its thongs, and this treatment was sometimes so severe that it killed those undergoing it. Thereafter, criminals were nailed to crosses, and if a modern experiment carried out in a hospital in Belgium some years ago on a corpse is anything to go by, the physical effects of this could only have been extremely damaging. When the experiment was made, it was soon discovered that nails driven through the palms of the hands did not hold the weight of a normal body; the hands split, and the body fell. It is probable therefore that the earliest tradition is right, and that nails were driven through a condemned man's wrists and feet, thus securing him to the cross in a position which, after a time, would have led to dislocation of the joints. On top of this, a crucified man would have lost much blood, suffered appalling pain, and lasted a short time only before dying of exhaustion. In John's Gospel, it is said that there came a time when Jesus was so obviously dead that the Roman soldiers attending his execution did not bother to hurry matters by breaking his legs, and although the other Gospels do not mention this, and it may have been included for theological reasons, it is highly unlikely that Roman soldiers, who were very used to killing people, would have left the scene or allowed anyone to take down a body from a cross until they were quite sure that the man was dead. But even if by some remarkable chance this had happened, those who wrapped the body of Jesus in grave clothes and placed it in the tomb would surely have noticed that he was still alive if there had been a flicker of life left in him. But if by some even more remarkable chance they had failed to do so, a man subjected to such appalling physical treatment and with half the joints in his body dislocated could not possibly have revived in the tomb, stood up, rolled away a stone weighing half a ton or more, and subsequently walked about the town in search of his friends.

The second suggestion sometimes made is that the disciples were subject to delusions; they did not really see Jesus, they only imagined they did. But this does not bear very much examination. Although the individual descriptions by the four Evangelists and St Paul of the events connected with the resurrection vary as much in detail and presentation as my imaginary pictures of Mont Ste Victoire by different artists, all of them agree that after his death Jesus appeared on some occasions to individuals or pairs of individuals, and on others he appeared to the disciples when they were all together. While the suggestion is credible enough that one or more of the disciples might very well have suffered delusions as a result of the fear and strain of the preceding days, the fact that several of them independently of each other and yet more or less simultaneously should have suffered exactly the same kind of delusions – that there should have been a sudden epidemic of identical delusions – is not easy to believe; and when the fact is added that Jesus is said to have appeared more than once to all of them together and no one cried, 'The Emperor's clothes! There is no one there. You are seeing things', I find the outbreak of such a remarkable unanimity of visual and aural hallucinations impossible to accept.

As far as I know, the only other suggested explanation of the behaviour of the disciples at Easter is that the whole thing was a deliberate fraud on their part; they or some of their friends stole and hid the body of Jesus and then proclaimed that God had raised him from the dead and that they had seen him and spoken to him. Whatever may be thought of the other suggestions, this one is not acceptable, for the nature of a fraud is that those who perpetrate it should gain something by doing so, and all the disciples gained for themselves by sticking to their story was the hatred of the authorities, persecution, and in several cases death by martyrdom. No one stands by a fraudulent story to the point of dying for it.

Which leaves only the explanation given by the disciples themselves that God had raised Jesus from the dead and had given them such convincing evidence of this that both they and their world had been turned upside down: evidence which, whether we like it or not, is embedded in the stories of the empty tomb, the resurrection appearances and the birth of faith in the earliest Church. I say 'whether we like it or not', though probably I should have said, 'although we do not like it at all'; for it is not our kind of evidence. We should much prefer a dossier of bare facts, with no inconsistencies, carefully compiled by a trained observer, who, if he were alive today, would be welcome as a contributor to the *American Historical Review* or, perhaps even better, to the *Westdeutsche Zeitschrift für Geschichte*; whereas what we have got are four verbal portraits of the events of that crucial time, together with a commentary upon them by St Paul: four portraits of events painted by four very different people and as full of differences – 'inconsistencies' if you like – as any four different portraits of the same subject will inevitably be. Moreover, what makes the stories of the resurrection contained in these verbal portraits even less satisfactory from our point of view – or anyway the point of view of the twentieth century – is that they give a strong impression of being stories not so much about hard facts as about a series of events, many of which are not patient of verbal description or prosaic analysis. There are exceptions; for instance, we are told that the tomb was empty, the body of Jesus gone, and that on one occasion the risen Christ ate broiled fish with his disciples: all apparently hard facts about the physical absence or presence of the risen Christ; but these reports of hard, intelligible facts are indeed excep-

tions. The majority of the stories of the resurrection
appearances seem to deal with much stranger events
than that. 'When the doors were shut for fear of the
Jews, Jesus came and stood in the midst', it is said in
John's Gospel, and that does not sound like a normal
entrance. In Luke's Gospel, the strangeness of the risen
Christ is even more strongly emphasized in the story of
the encounter on the road to Emmaus, when two disciples meet a man they do not know, walk to the village
with him, conversing on the way, sit down in the local
inn to a meal with him, and only then quite suddenly
'their eyes were opened, and they knew him; and he
vanished out of their sight'. Similarly, when Peter and
four other disciples were fishing on the sea of Tiberias,
Jesus appeared on the shore and called to them, but they
did not recognize him; only later did they do so, and
even then 'none of the disciples dared to ask him, Who
are you? They knew it was the Lord'. And so I could go
on; but the fact is that we do not know precisely what
happened in hard physical fact. The event which transformed the lives of the disciples and eventually over-
turned the world refuses to be laid out on the dissecting
table for scientific examination and precise historical
analysis; but that does not mean that we are left with
nothing at all. On the contrary, something must have
happened so to transform the disciples, and what we are
left with is the explosion of faith which that 'something',
whatever it may have been, caused.

Paul called that 'something' an act of new creation on
God's part. As a result of the resurrection, he told the
Corinthians that 'if any man is in Christ, he is a new
creature; the old has passed away, behold, all things are
become new.' The explosion of faith in God through
Christ was the result of this act of new creation by means
of which every human being could be taken up into a

new life and a new world of faith, hope and charity. I know that the worlds of Pauline theology and modern cosmology are distinct, but I am not convinced that human knowledge is so locked up in closed and separate compartments that the contents of one may not serve to illuminate that of another; and modern science has changed so much in our own time that in some ways its paradigms are more like theological analogies than the old mechanistic models of nineteenth-century science, and I believe that the one realm may indeed serve today to illuminate the other, if only because they sometimes face very similar difficulties and embarrassments. As a case in point, Sir Bernard Lovell, speaking in 1975 of the origin of the universe, pointed out that 'the striking observational evidence that 10,000 million years ago the universe was beginning to evolve from a dense concentrate of primeval material ... presents us with an imponderable conceptual difficulty'; for although 'the solution of the equations of general relativity provide us with expanding models for the universe evolving from zero radius at the beginning of time ... the great difficulty is that these evolutionary models for the universe inevitably predict a singular condition of infinite density of infinitesimal dimensions before the beginning of the expansion' and, incidentally, before the existence of space. This is literally inconceivable; we can make no mental image of it, and yet the observational evidence of the expanding universe all round us filled, as it is, with isotropic radiation left over as a relic of the Big Bang, makes it impossible to deny that at the beginning of time the universe must have existed in such a state of infinite density and yet zero size: everything in nothing, in fact; and 'this,' as Sir Bernard acknowledges, 'is an embarrassing situation for science', which does not like such conceptual impossibilities.

Nor does theology, for that matter, but when dealing with the ultimate mystery of God it is not always possible to avoid embarrassment; and it is not entirely surprising that in both the old and the new creations, if that is indeed what the beginning of the universe and the resurrection of Christ really were, we are confronted with just such difficulties; and yet in both the observed results are indisputable. We may never know how everything was produced out of nothing in the Big Bang, or what the spirit of God, brooding in the darkness of the tomb, did to the broken body of Jesus; but as we know that the expanding universe exists, so we know too that there was a great explosion of faith in Palestine at the beginning of our era which has gone on expanding throughout the world ever since, and all accounts agree that it arose because the disciples were given evidence that God had raised Jesus from the dead. That this presents Christians with 'an imponderable conceptual difficulty' is undeniable, but since no one has ever put forward a credible alternative to account for the explosion of faith at Easter I agree with Clifford Longley, the religious correspondent of *The Times*, who has said that 'if explanations biased against faith are at the end of the day thoroughly unconvincing, an explanation in the light of faith becomes almost unavoidable.'

Indeed, at this point I should like to go further and say that, in the absence of any reasonable alternative to the disciples' own story to account for what Paul called the 'new creation', it is not unreasonable to believe that, if there is a God at all, and if Jesus was in any way right to believe what he believed about him, God had little alternative but to show someone that death had not been the end of him; for otherwise no one could have escaped the conclusion that he, Jesus, had been a sadly mistaken religious fanatic who had thrown away a highly talented life in the grip of a monstrous delusion, and that trust in God was therefore a policy for fools. Although this conviction of mine is expressed, as all religious convictions and statements must be expressed, in the language of metaphor and analogy rather than in the prosaic terms of material description, I still believe it to be reasonable; but I am well aware, too, that such a belief transcends reason. Reason alone did not take me by the hand and lead me to belief in the resurrection of Christ any more than reason opened my ears to the splendour of Allegri's *Miserere* the first time I heard it, or stopped me in my tracks in front of Uccello's *Rout of San Romano* in my student days, and I do not expect reasonable argument about the evidence in the New Testament to persuade anyone to believe in the resurrection any more than it persuaded me.

For the fact is that, as in the first days of the new creation, so today no one recognizes the risen Christ until he chooses to reveal himself. Belief is the result of a self-disclosure by God, as Paul knew when he told the citizens of Corinth that 'no man can say, Jesus is Lord, but by the Holy Spirit'. That sounds dauntingly pious, but I think that it is the language of conversion and belief, tarnished as it has been by religious commercialism with its professional ad-men who, no doubt with the best of intentions, try to sell Christian conversion as if it were a patent medicine, packaged in clichés and guaranteed to kill all known germs, which is putting off. The experience itself is simply that of discovering that one believes something one did not believe before, and although such a discovery can be dramatic – as dramatic occasionally as Otto Loewi's experience in the field of scientific discovery – often it is not so. I am not even sure *when* I discovered that I believed that God had raised Christ from the dead, but, as I have already said, I

certainly did not come to believe it as a result of studying
the evidence in a scholarly way; on the contrary, I
turned to the evidence afterwards in order to see how
tenable belief in the resurrection might be, rather, I
suppose, as Otto Loewi put the inspiration which had
come to him in his sleep to the test when he eventually
woke up and found it already planted in his head. Belief
is the result of disclosure rather than the culmination of
a rational process, though whatever it may be which is
disclosed should be subjected to rational examination
and criticism after the event.

Although I know this to be the case, and I accept it,
like an old computer programmed years ago, I am still
sufficiently conditioned by the largely unquestioned
assumptions of our own day with its worship of reason
(however unreasonably it may constantly behave) to
feel slightly embarrassed when admitting this. Similarly, when I find as illustrious a twentieth-century
philosopher as Martin Heidegger, once of Freiburg
University, saying that 'thinking only begins at the
point where we have come to know that Reason,
glorified for centuries, is the most obstinate adversary of
thinking', all the old hackles on my ex-atheist-rationalist
back rise up, and I bristle like one of Pavlov's dogs; but
if Heidegger meant that our existence, our being, in all
its earthy richness and varied capability cannot be
neatly fitted into the theoretical concepts which have
been fashioned for special use in the realm of pure
reason, he is plainly right. When God irrupts into 'this
world' in the creation of the universe or into its rich and
earthy existence in the resurrection of Christ, or even
indeed into my earthy existence or your earthy existence, I can only agree with Immanuel Kant that 'pure
reason' cannot be stretched to tame and cage such
events.

The same point has been better made at the end of that most splendidly rational of books in the Old Testament, in which Job takes on God in a dogged argument and refuses to give up until the outer limits of argumentation and reason have been reached; then and only then is Job confronted with the reality of God and his power in a whirlwind, as astronomy is confronted with God and his power in the Big Bang, and as the disciples were confronted with the reality of God and his power in the resurrection of Christ from the dead; and then and only then Job said, 'I know that thou canst do all things, and that no purpose of thine can be restrained. Who is this that hideth counsel without knowledge? Therefore I have utterly abhorred that which I understood not, things too wonderful for me that I knew not. Hear, I beseech thee, and I will speak; I will demand of thee, and declare thou unto me. I had heard of thee by the hearing of the ear; but now mine eye seeth thee, wherefore I abhor myself, and repent in dust and ashes.'

IX

The Images of Birth

In the previous chapter I ran ahead of myself, and I must now return to the subject of the birth of belief. Some converts to the Christian faith tell me that the truth burst on them like a great star-shell, illuminating the landscape of their lives in a moment of time with such a flood of divine light that they felt as though they had been born again into a new world and that they have never felt the same since that moment. If there is any truth in the old saying that it takes all sorts to make a world, then it probably takes more than one kind of convert to make a Church; but however that may be, I certainly did not become a Christian in such a spectacular way. Instead, as I have said, Christianity crept up on me, breaking and entering the unoccupied apartment of my head like a squatter almost before I noticed that it had been invaded, and getting to know the new occupant was a gradual process; indeed, to begin with I refused to recognize the existence of such a despised and unwelcome intruder, and it was only slowly over many months that I began to understand and respect him. But although my experience was very different from that of those who call themselves 'born again' Christians, I understand how they feel, and I respect their sincerity and the depth of their conviction; but there are, I think, aspects of their particular brand of Christian fervour which can be counter-productive in commending Christianity to some people. For instance, it is often associated with a purblind biblical fundamentalism, which is not made more appealing by the unwavering assurance of its adherents that they and only they are the possessors and guardians of God's truth. Yet the experiences of renewal, to which the great images of birth and rebirth in Christian belief and symbolism point, do not lead all those to whom they occur to embrace that kind of religious totalitarianism.

Rebirth means renewal, and St Paul spoke of all things being made new rather than of personal renewal alone. 'If any man is in Christ,' he reminded the Corinthian church, 'he is a new creature; the old has passed away; behold, all things are become new.' Being a new creature is much the same as being born again, but Paul widens the concept to embrace all things, and this made sense to me. Gradually, as the results of what had happened to me made themselves felt, the old world in which I had lived revealed itself to be a different place from that which I had always believed it to be: a place shot through with different implications and perspectives and loaded with hints I had never noticed. Curiously enough, in trying to describe this experience of a transformed world, it was science which came to my rescue; for the nearest I have ever come to finding my own experience at this time analysed in detail and beautifully described came when I was reading Kuhn's book, *The Structure of Scientific Revolutions*, to which I have already referred; writing about the results of a change of world view in science comparable to the changes inaugurated by such men as Copernicus, Newton and Einstein, Kuhn observed that

led by a new paradigm, scientists adopt new instruments and look in new places. Even more important, during revolutions scientists see new and different things when looking with familiar instruments in places they have looked before. It is rather as if the professional community had been suddenly transported to a different planet where familiar objects are seen in a different light and are joined by unfamiliar ones as well. Of course, nothing of quite that sort does occur: there is no geographical transplantation; outside the laboratory everyday affairs usually continue as before. Nevertheless, paradigm changes do cause scientists to see the world of their research-engagement differently. In so far as their only recourse to that world is through what they see and do, we may want to say that after a revolution scientists are responding to a different world.

We may indeed want to say just that. I did, and the fact that the world was a different place with new dimensions to explore – or, perhaps more accurately, that the old familiar world had been transformed – was both startling and invigorating.

But it was not entirely unprecedented, because for many years I had been aware of the fact that transformation was an inherent part of works of art: aware, indeed, if only vaguely, that one of the prime characteristics of great works of art was that they revealed the transcendent splendour of essentially ordinary things, though I had not thought this out or put it into words. But from the days of the cave painters of Lascaux and Altamira with their wild horses, bison and deer, through the octopuses on Minoan vases and the birds on Pharaonic walls, up past Rembrandt's old Jews, Breughel's bucolic dancing peasants and the little children of Louis le Nain to our own time with Cézanne's apples and Renoir's irresistible naked girls, the stuff of great works of art has been ordinariness transformed. In Peter Shaffer's play, *Amadeus*, the court musician, Salieri, bemoans the fact that, whereas the genius of a man like Mozart is to transform the ordinary into the miraculous, it is his fate to transform the miraculous into the all-too-ordinary hack music of the court. But although I had vaguely realized for years that such was the nature of the arts at their best, the fact that Christian belief was founded on an experience of the ordinary world transformed in much the same way as the world glimpsed by artists came as a total surprise to me. The greatest transformation of them all, of course, was the transformation of the very ordinarily dead Jesus into the living Christ: that is to say, the result of the act of new creation and transformation glimpsed by the disciples and formative as the agent of their own transformation and that of their world, as it is still the active agent in transforming the lives of those today who get a glimpse of the same dead man, raised and renewed by God — hence all the talk of rebirth. Although the comparison will seem unforgivably trivial to some people, I was forcibly reminded of how Uccello's self-disclosure had opened up an entirely new world to me years before and of how enormously enriching that experience had been. The self-disclosure of God through Christ, of course, was vastly more so.

Indeed, the consequences of the fact that God is self-disclosing, and that the initiative in the divine–human conversation is his not ours, are revolutionary. As I came to recognize them, they completed the transformation, if not of me myself, of the notional landscape in which I found myself living. The first and most obvious of these consequences was that the concept of self-sufficiency, which lies at the heart of humanism, began to look sick and absurd, while the splendid epiphytic growth of human pride, which depends upon it as a tropical orchid depends upon its host, began to look dangerously attractive like some exotic and deadly poisonous plants. I don't, of course, mean that my own pride and self-esteem died like weeds before the flame-thrower of God's unexpected advent; I remain as subject to recurrent attacks of both as a chronic asthmatic is subject to fits of breathlessness, but at least at this time I began to recognize that such attacks were symptoms of a disease. Indeed, perhaps I should have said *the* disease, for the attempt to justify ourselves in our own eyes, which occupies most of us most of the time, together with our attempts to manufacture some sort of significance for our lives in the eyes of others by achieving success in one field or another, lies at the root of most of our individual and corporate frustrations, self-inflicted wounds and destructive rivalries. Yet, plainly enough, if there is any sense in the idea that we stand in relationship to God as children to their father, our various efforts at self-justification are as pathetic and as unnecessary as the antics adopted by children to impress their parents.

It is conventional to go on from there to denounce the self as the villain of the piece and all self-regarding desires as evil; but this, I think, is dangerous nonsense. On the contrary, self-fulfilment – the blossoming of the self – is the right and proper consummation of each individual life; the only problem is how to achieve it, and if the evidence of either history or personal frustration is anything to go by, aggressive self-assertion over against other people, either by means of corporate violence or by means of personal, financial or psychological dominance, is not the way to do so; it seldom leads to much lasting satisfaction. Violence provokes violence, and most people who live corporately by the sword do, as a matter of history, eventually die by the sword, either tribally, nationally or culturally; while those who pin their hopes of personal fulfilment to the bandwagon of financial success or some other kind of dominance generally discover before they die that the saying 'Man does not live by bread alone' is not mere pious nonsense, as most of us assume in our hard-headed youth, but descriptive of a harsh reality, as the zest of wealth dies in a thin and rather barren old age.

Meanwhile, from a religious point of view, self-assertion has an even more malodorous and murderous historical record than that chalked up by *homo profanus* down the ages, and this is not surprising; for religious people have greatly outnumbered unbelievers in the past. The heart of religious self-assertion is the belief that people can lift themselves by their own boot-laces and make themselves acceptable to God, becoming in the process not only the sole repositories of God's truth but better than everyone else; whereas the truth is that those who believe themselves to be successful in this endeavour become riddled with hubris, which is the stuff of religious failure, while those who fail in the same endeavour do indeed fail; and thus the enterprise is doomed to failure whatever happens. In fact, at a deeper level it is bound to fail, for the attempt at self-justification and self-enthronement over against self-forgetfulness and self-abandonment to the springs and wells of life is the root of most of our personal frustrations and miseries and many of the evils of the world in which we live, let alone the origin of alienation from God.

That is a dogmatic statement, but it receives support from two widely separated and somewhat improbable sources: from the works of that remarkable German—American polymath, Paul Tillich, and from the old biblical myth of Adam and Eve, which received such scornful treatment at the hands of the intellectual *avant-garde* in the nineteenth century. The heart of that timeless insight into the human condition is to be found in Eve's encounter with the serpent, an animal with death in its mouth, which tempts her to believe that

God is a liar and that she herself, the mother of all humanity, can become like God if only she will disobey him and eat the forbidden fruit of the tree of the knowledge of good and evil: that is to say, in biblical and mythological terms, God's knowledge. Thus, in the biblical myth, succumbing to the temptation to enthrone oneself as God and arrogating to oneself the divine moral omniscience is identified as the root of our trouble; and perhaps it is permissible to ask whether the 'moment' in evolutionary mythology, when a member of the race, *Australopithecus*, or whichever hominoid ape I must regard with filial gratitude as my distant ancestor, achieved self-consciousness, was also the 'moment' in our aboriginal journey down from the Darwinian tree-tops, when we became human as opposed to being merely simian? And if so, was self-enthronement or the tendency thereto – self-reliance and self-sufficiency – born in us at the same moment? In mythical terms, this could be put as the question, 'Was the possibility of self-idolatry the risk that God took when he made men and women to be the first animals to know the kind of self-consciousness which he himself knew?' If the answer is 'Yes!', then the Fall was simultaneous with the Creation, and human alienation is endemically human: very original sin in fact.

But if the realization that 'we are not sufficient of ourselves to think anything as of ourselves' lays an axe to the root of the tree of human self-esteem, for the true self it has some marvellously liberating consequences, which have been analysed in depth by Paul Tillich. The New Testament in general and St Paul in particular describes them in terms of freedom from sin, but since the various Churches have reduced and perverted the concept of sin to that of breaching any one of a number of moral rules, dwelling with particular relish and feroc-

ity upon the rules governing sexual behaviour, understandably the world has rejected the idea of sin
altogether, preferring to use less compromised words to
describe the vagaries of human behaviour. Tillich contended that to be human at all, as opposed to being a
cockatoo or a sea-slug, was to suffer from three built-in
anxieties which, if left unattended, were liable to
become neurotic and thus to undermine the individual
lives of many men and women and also the corporate
lives of whole societies, cultures and civilizations: anxieties over meaninglessness, guilt and not-being have
stalked through human history like a trinity of furies,
according to Tillich, and it is difficult not to agree with
him. I have already looked briefly at the abundant
evidence of a corrosive anxiety besetting many people
today that life may be without meaning, purpose or
value, an anxiety which is not made any the less persist-
ent by the kind of lifestyle which is forced on most of us
by the urbanized mass society of the industrialized,
secularized nations, both of the capitalist West and the
communist East. Tillich's allegation that guilt still
threatens the peace of humanity must also be considered, if only because many people seem to believe that
Freud has delivered us all from its clutches and no one
suffers its destructive ravages any more. This is not true
even as far as sexual guilt is concerned, though happily
condemnation of other people's sexual behaviour is no
longer either as fashionable or as vicious as it often was
in the past; but lapses from the accepted sexual norms of
behaviour are not the only causes of guilt, and both
individually and, even more so, corporately people
today show every sign of feeling, if only half-consciously,
guilty for their past economic and military sins, or for
the sins of their fathers and forefathers; guilty for the
treatment meted out to coloured and colonial peoples,

guilty for the social oppression and exploitation of the
poor and under-privileged slum-dwellers of the
nineteenth century, guilty for the bombs, both atomic
and otherwise, which wiped out the Hamburgs, Dres-
dens, Hiroshimas and Nagasakis of the immediate past,
and guilty at the remembrance of the camps at such
places as Auschwitz and Treblinka. I have no doubt that
practising psychiatrists could easily add a large number
of other common causes of personal guilt to the list, as
they could also dwell at length on the various ways in
which we try to hide or deny them under cloaks of
aggression or anger, or off-load them on to some con-
venient scapegoat: God, for instance, for why did he
create such a bloody world in the first place? Or the
Jews, the Fascists or the long-suffering Reds under
those familiar beds; but I am not a psychiatrist, and I
must leave the list to them.

One does not need to be a psychiatrist, however, to
agree with Tillich that anxiety over the prospect of
annihilation – of not-being – is endemically human. It is
not the same thing as the fear of death, which is shared
by all animals when their lives are threatened; on such
occasions, our stomachs turn over, we sweat, tremble,
feel like evacuating our bowels and bladders to lighten
ourselves for flight, breathe more rapidly than usual and
are aware of our hearts pumping away for dear life. All
mammals react to danger in a similar way but, as far as I
know, no other animal lies awake at night, as we all do
from time to time, unable to sleep because we know that
the membrane which separates us from the abyss of
not-being is so thin that it may rupture at any moment
with the breaking of a blood-vessel or the blocking of an
artery. Swinburne, in his lyrical tragedy *Atalanta in
Calydon*, painted a portrait of man in thrall to this kind
of angry human anxiety:

His speech is a burning fire;
    With his lips he travaileth;
In his heart is a blind desire,
    In his eyes foreknowledge of death;
He weaves, and is clothed with derision;
    Sows, and he shall not reap;
His life is a watch or a vision
    Between a sleep and a sleep.

Tillich contended that certain ages were corporately dominated by one or other of these three endemic human anxieties more than by the others, and he cited as examples the obsession with death of the Graeco–Roman world of late antiquity as manifested in the pullulation of religious sects and mystery religions, including Christianity, which promised immortality to their initiates, and the equally obvious obsession with unresolved guilt of the medieval world of Europe with its flagellant sects, penitential asceties and stylites, sale of pardons and indulgences, and morbid preoccupation with hell fire. It is easy enough in historical retrospect to agree with these examples, but it is much more difficult to go on to decide whether our own age is dominated more by meaninglessness, death or unresolved guilt, or whether it is in equal servitude to all three; but certainly individuals today have to cope with their own anxieties with very little help from anyone, since the Churches shattered most people's trust in Christianity by centuries of fratricidal strife, corruption and legalism, and since humanism was murdered by the re-emergence and triumph of barbarism in the years between 1914 and 1918 and again in those which followed 1939. Yet those anxieties are as lively today as they have ever been, and I believe that much of our hectic and relentlessly noisy lifestyle is the result of an attempt to stifle them with trivia. Philip Larkin has nailed this particular modern syndrome to the wall for public exhibition in his poem, *Vers de Société*:

> *My wife and I have asked a crowd of craps*
> *To come and waste their time and ours: perhaps*
> *You'd care to join us? In a pig's arse, friend.*
> Day comes to an end.
> The gas fire breathes, the trees are darkly swayed.
> And so *Dear Warlock-Williams: I'm afraid—*
>
> Funny how hard it is to be alone.
> I could spend half my evenings, if I wanted,
> Holding a glass of washing sherry, canted
> Over to catch the drivel of some bitch
> Who's reading nothing but *Which*;
> Just think of all the spare time that has flown
>
> Straight into nothingness by being filled
> With forks and faces, rather than repaid
> Under a lamp, hearing the noise of the wind,
> And looking out to see the moon thinned
> To an air-sharpened blade.

But the process of killing time in case, if we allow it to live, it may force us to think, begins long before our carefully arranged and vapid social evenings; we wake in the morning, turn on a transistor radio, read a paper at breakfast and perhaps another on the bus, tube or commuter train as we go to work, or even don ear-phones to ensure that our minds are numb with noise from pocket radios: we work ourselves silly all day with a break for gossip, a drink and lunch in a pub or a burger-bar with background music from a radio or juke-box dutifully blaring, return home in the late afternoon with an evening paper, eat, watch the television or play bridge or go to a party with the Warlock-Williamses; finally we have a night-cap or a sleeping pill or both and thus retire to bed having banished all possibility of allowing Tillich's imprisoned demons to break the surface of our dreams. But keeping them caged in the dungeons of the unconscious mind only makes them angrier and more insistent than ever, and so we double our activity, increase the dose of noise and alcohol, 'Stiffen the sinews, summon up the blood, Disguise fair nature with hard favour'd rage', and dedicate ourselves afresh to proving to ourselves and others that such anxieties do not bother us, for ours is the kingdom, the power and the glory, for ever and ever, Amen. Eventually, of course, the demons win, even if they have to wait to do so until they have culti-vated an ulcer in our duodenum worthy of a prize in the local ulcer show or perhaps a terminally splendid coro-nary thrombosis to make us realize that if we refuse to release our demonic anxieties and face them they will destroy us.

At this point it would be all too easy to insist in a fine flurry of enthusiasm that the heart of Christian experi-ence is to be freed from these three demonic human anxieties by the knowledge of the love of God which is implicit in the resurrection of Christ as the culmina-tion of his self-disclosure; and so, indeed, it is. For forgiveness is the key to freedom from guilt, and finding oneself accepted and loved constitutes the stuff of for-giveness, while the discovery that one has been created for an eternal destiny, however unimaginable that des-tiny may be, dispels any idea that our lives may be meaningless and cuts away the ground upon which our anxiety over not-being used to rest; but while all this is true and liberating we are creatures of habit, and old ways of life and thought do not die overnight. Like

Pavlov's dogs, many of our actions and reactions are conditioned reflexes over which we exercise little conscious control; years of striving to make ourselves acceptable to ourselves and others shape and form the patterns of our behaviour, which, once fashioned, are doggedly resistant to change, and traces of the old anxieties linger on in the subterranean chambers of our minds like smoke left over from last night's drunken party.

This can have various results; the man whose new belief and outlook are principally a matter of intellectual assent to the proposition that, because the initiative is God's and Advent is forever, he may relax in the knowledge of God's love and cast off the shackles of the old anxieties can become so excited by his new-found freedom from anxiety that he enthrones his own intellectual conviction in the place of God, worships it, and determines never to be unfaithful to it or change it by one iota; it is the truth, and he has it. Thus, with his mind firmly closed, he exchanges one idolatry for another and spends the rest of his life relying, not on God, but on his own particular doctrine of God, while the man whose conversion is principally the result of an emotional experience is often even more unyielding, if less intelligent, than his intellectual counterpart. I realize that this is much too harsh a judgement, and that I probably make it because I myself fell into a similar trap for a time and was rescued only by the grace and patience of various friends, of whom John Fenton, the biblical theologian and Canon of Oxford, was perhaps the most influential and helpful. But even if such a judgement is too harsh, I make no apology for making it, for the trap is real and the bait which lures people into it is so attractive that the churches are filled with people who have been caught by it. The bait, of course, is certitude:

the knowledge that you are the possessor of all truth, while other people wallow in their ignorance with the exception of those who agree with you; and nothing is more enjoyable than that. But the price people pay for such a possession is exorbitant; for the promise in the gospel is not that those who are 'born again' shall receive the truth, lock, stock and barrel as a christening present, but that they shall be freed from the old chains of self-idolatry and self-justification to be led into all truth by the spirit of God, whose direction, like that of the wind, can be predicted by no one. You cannot be led into the truth, however, if you are sitting on it, and if the windy spirit of God is to lead you in unpredictable ways you must be free to follow wherever you may be led. It is better, I suppose, to be born into the nursery and never to move out of it than never to be born at all, but it seems to me to be better still to recognize that birth is the beginning of a new life, not the end, and that growing up involves change. If the freedom and possibility of self-fulfilment, of which the notion of new birth in Christian imagery is the symbolic beginning, are to become lasting realities, they must embrace the freedom to ask all questions and raise all objections; and one or two such questions and objections clamour for attention.

X

Some Objections

I think it was Peter Ustinov, on being elected Rector of a Scottish University, who remarked that, if the time ever came when there were no more questions left to be asked, because men and women had at last discovered all the answers, the only course open to a reasonable person would be to commit suicide. I know what he means, for when I meet churchmen – or Communists or humanists for that matter – who claim to have all the answers to all the problems of being alive, they induce something very like suicidal tendencies in me with greater speed than anything else. As far as churchmen are concerned, I long to confront them with the mother of a child of three or four years of age who has just been told that her daughter has an inoperable cancer and will last with luck for a few painful months before dying, and ask them, '*Why?*'; and if this question fails to shake their trust in their own omniscience, I should like to make them write an essay on the theology of the malarial mosquito or alternatively a thesis on the divine purpose in the creation of *pasteurella pestis*, the bacillus which causes bubonic plague. The problems to which Christians have no complete or satisfactory answers are numerous, and it is essential to say so; for not only is our ignorance obvious to everyone else, but to admit it may lead us into a further examination of those problems in the hope that at least we may be able to make some sort of contribution to their understanding, even if we cannot solve them.

Obviously, within the short compass of this book I cannot possibly look at all the problems posed by belief in God or discuss all the objections which people might wish to raise against it; but I do want to glance briefly at the two greatest impediments to religious belief in general and Christian belief in particular which bothered me for years, and indeed still do so: namely, the existence of suffering and the record and behaviour of the Church. They are not new problems. Job wrestled with the problem of how to reconcile the fact of human suffering to the idea of a just and loving God, and it has not disappeared since Job's day; and as for the Church, at times it seems as if the best that can be said for it is that it must have some hidden purpose in the providence of God, or he would have destroyed it centuries ago. Yet the paradoxical fact must also be recognized, simply because it is a fact, that God is more often reached – or, rather, people are more often reached by God – through and beyond the rationally indefensible experience of suffering and the manifest absurdity of a worldly, legalistic, bickering and recurrently obscurantist Church than in any other ways. For both suffering and the Church are two-sided; they can be seen in two apparently incompatible ways, suffering as the Siamese twin of love, and the Church as the point in time and space where the love of God meets the failure of man.

The Church's sins of commission and omission have been so numerous down the ages that it would be impossible to make an adequate list of them here, and they are so well-documented that such a monumental labour of distaste would in any case be unnecessary. Moreover, it could be argued that there is no point in raking up old scandals, since the past is the past, and having lost much of its old political and economic power in most parts of the world the Church no longer indulges in the more spectacular crimes with which it occupied itself in the old days; religious wars, burnings, persecutions, anathemas and the like are now more typical of Communists and certain Moslems than of Christians, though in Ireland and Lebanon tribal groups with denominational labels still bring religion into disrepute with their crimes of violence. But despite these exceptions, most churchmen today would contend that the Church is different from what it used to be in the bad old days. Up to a point, I agree, but there is one respect in which the Church has not changed at all. All down the ages, while claiming to be a divine institution, filled and led by the Spirit of God and with no abiding citizenship in this world, the Church, like some deathless chameleon, has taken on the colour of whatever worldly society it has happened to find itself in at the time, while indulging in most of the sins and crimes typical of the age; and it has never done this more thoroughly than today. In Byzantine days it could scarcely have been more imperial than it was, supporting the various Emperors in their passion to maintain the unity of their huge and potentially fissiparous realm by persecuting internal dissent with implacable orthodox ferocity and launching what would now be called imperialist missions to bring the Empire's non-Christian neighbours into line by ideological conversion. A little later, in feudal days, the Church was so much part of its parent society that many of the cathedrals built at this time closely resemble castles, while bishops' palaces actually were castles in all but name, and the bishops themselves, like their secular counterparts the barons, as often as not could be seen on horseback with their swords red with the blood of the enemies of Christendom, whether they happened to be Turks, Saracens or Mameluks. Times changed, however, and as the aristocratic seventeenth century in France passed smoothly into the eighteenth, Saint-Simon recorded in his *Memoirs* how, on one occasion, the chaplain to the Duke of Rohan was obliged to inform his lord and master that owing to a most unfortunate oversight the special wafers impressed with the ducal arms and used at Mass to communicate His Grace had run out, and inquired in fear and some trembling whether the Duke would be willing for once to take pot luck with the common people. Meanwhile, the situation was not so very different in England where, it has been said, a typical eighteenth-century Anglican bishop had one thing and one thing only in common with Almighty God, namely that one could say of both the one and the other that 'no man hath seen him at any time'. Later still, in Victorian days the English Church taught its children to sing of God's wisdom in creating the rich man in his castle and the poor man at his gate, while sending legions of missionaries overseas as the spiritual arm of colonialism to convert the heathen in his blindness to a proper appreciation of the benefits of British rule.

Far from renouncing this kind of social conformism or abdicating its role as chameleon, nowadays the Church has transformed itself into a bureaucratic annexe to the Welfare State with a few pious and neo-Gothic overtones. Hag-ridden by committees and worm-eaten by synodical government, it has dedicated itself to activism, having banished prayer, mystery, silence, beauty and its own rich musical and liturgical heritage to a few remote oases in order to make way for hymns written by third-rate disciples of Noël Coward and sung to the strident noise of guitars played by charismatic curates in jeans; it is wedded, too, to the letter of a restrictive moral code and neglectful of the spirit, while confusing chumminess and post-

Communion coffee with the love of God and the
fellowship of the Holy Spirit, and is so rooted and
grounded in this world that to use the words 'other
worldly' has become a social and doctrinal solecism. In
politics the Church frowns on extremes and makes it
virtually compulsory for churchmen to be wishy-washy
pink but with true blue edges. Rumour has it that Sir
Steven Runciman, depressed by this Gadarene stam-
pede of the Western Churches into the secular sea all
round them, has prophesied that the Orthodox Church
will be the only Church left in fifty years time, and when
I survey the contemporary ecclesiastical scene, I am
sometimes tempted to fear, not that he may be right but
that he may be wrong.

And yet, in a supremely paradoxical way, these recurrent and abysmal idiocies of the Church, ridiculous here
on earth, can also be grounds for hope and reassurance:
hope because, despite the fact that they have indeed
been recurrent down the ages, there are still nearly two
thousand million Christians in the world, and reassur-
ing because Christianity is not about the creation of a
faultless community of idealists, judged to be perfect by
the standards of this world, but about the transformation by the grace and love of God of ordinary men and
women who know that they are not sufficient of themselves to think anything as of themselves, but hope and
trust that in the end their sufficiency may be of God.
When I remember this and look again at the world's
idealists and their self-assured communities, I fall in
love with the Church all over again, warts and all, for
there seems to me to be nothing in the world more
lethally dangerous than a bunch of dedicated idealists;
as Professor John Passmore remarked in his book, *The
Perfectibility of Man*, (1970):

They set out in search of a total order, a total harmony, and neither science nor art, as Plato saw and the dystopians have seen after him, could be freely operating within such a total order; science and art are by their very nature revolutionary, destructive of established orders. Perfectibilists tell us not only to abandon our possessions but to abandon our loves; to be not merely dispassionate but, what is very different, without passion; to seek a kind of unity which is destructive of that diversity which is the glory of the world and the secret of all man's achievements; to be self-sufficient in a sense which does not permit of love.

He might have added that dedicated idealists are also perhaps the most frequent advocates of violence as a means of achieving whatever ideal political ends they may happen to cherish. Certainly, the worst crimes committed by Christians have nearly always been perpetrated in the name of God and in furtherance of some lofty ecclesiastical ideal – the truth, the purity of the faith, the unity of Christendom, the defeat of evil or the conversion of the heathen – while their greatest achievements have been the result of a vision vouchsafed to people like Francis of Assisi, John Wesley, William Wilberforce, Albert Schweitzer, and Mother Teresa of Calcutta: a vision of ordinary, fallible, muddled and messy human beings as images of God to be loved as they are and for what they are.

At this point, perhaps I should say in brief parenthesis that I did not join the Church, if that is the right way to describe being ordained into its ministry, for any very noble reasons or because I felt irresistibly called by God to do so. In fact, when it first crossed my mind that I might become a clergyman, the idea was so ludicrous that I dismissed it at once as a symptom of incipient religious mania. By this time, however, I suspected that as a painter I should never be a Rembrandt or a Rouault, and as the weeks and months went by and I heard appeals from the pulpit Sunday by Sunday for people to volunteer for the ministry, I found it progressively difficult to see any good reason why I should not at least offer myself; but since I could also see no good reason why I should do so, I remained in a state of indecision. Then, one day in the early 1950s after I had spent some time in silence in the London house of a monastic order of Anglican monks, I went to see my mother, who was recovering from a minor operation in a nursing home. I travelled on the top of a bus, and as it made its way up the Tottenham Court Road I was overcome by the same sort of experience that I had had years ago in the suburban train near Bromley; once again, the dingy landscape became transparent to something other than itself, and as I looked at the small forest of dreary Victorian church spires pointing upwards to the grey London sky over the desert of urban roof-tops which stretched away to the wrecked horizon, I knew that I had to identify myself with them. They were symbols of hope in a dry land: hope whether the people of London, for whom they pointed their stony fingers to God, knew it or not: hope that the ordinary men and women who lived there, like the London spires, were also pointers to God for those with eyes to see the hidden truth of them. When I told my wife that I had decided to offer myself for ordination, she sat down and asked me for a drink.

It is easy to speak of people as pointers to God, and for a moment or two on the bus, the people in the street below, like the sky-pointing spires of Bloomsbury and Euston above, seemed to be just that; but I do not want to give a false impression, and most of the time I do not find it easy to see people like that. That is a commentary on my own blindness, combined with the fact that true vision is a gift of God, but it is also a commentary, I think, upon the fact that people are unwilling to walk naked and unashamed in another person's presence if they can avoid doing so. Instead, they hide behind a social mask until such time as something happens to make them drop it for a moment or two: the death of a friend, a failure or a fear realized, the birth of a child or the blossoming of an unexpected love; at such times, the dullest of dull people may split open for a moment or two like a ripe fig to reveal the richness of the true person inside, and having once been given a glimpse of one dull person transformed, it is easier to see the truth of other people hidden behind their opaque protective masks and mimes. Such glimpses come the way of a clergyman more often, perhaps, than they do to many other people, and it is this which makes it easy every now and again to see the dull ranks of church people become filled with multitudes of mini-Mother-Teresas in shabby pews and dowdy hats, and pocket Wesleys and Wilberforces in tired, dilapidated cassocks. To adopt a different metaphor, rather as medieval stained glass looks grey and lifeless when viewed from outside a church building but from inside lights up in a great richness of colour and splendour of light when the sun comes out, the community of the Church is transformed from time to time when viewed from inside, as the grace of God comes out and illuminates it; from outside, too, the prayers and unnoticed acts of kindness of church people remain largely unseen, the one deemed useless and the other too ordinary to be worthy of attention, while their common acts of sacrifice and generosity and the hours of time given to the lost, the neurotic, the despairing, the suicidal and the other refugees from living, let alone to the just plain dull, remain hidden with them. Seen from inside, however, the Church is filled with little irruptions of God and his grace, redeeming its perpetual human failure and absurdity and transforming the lives of those who, having fallen through Koestler's trap-door, turn to it with its music, its ritual and the recurrent miracle of its little mouthfuls of bread and sips of wine, because they can think of nowhere better to turn; but perhaps the greatest transforming miracle of them all is not that the Church, viewed from inside, is seen from time to time to be filled with irruptions of God, but that the natural world looked at from inside the Church is also seen to be as full of traces of God as a dawn hedge is loud with the whistling of blackbirds, even though the world, like the hedge itself, is deaf to the love-song in its branches.

So much for the paradox of the Church with its long and infamous criminal record and its multitudinous and ever-present stupidities co-existing with its equally long and salutary role as the out-patients' department of heaven; but what about the unambiguously evil existence of suffering? Accused by a righteously indignant humanity of creating a world full of cancer, multiple sclerosis, earthquakes, famines, wars and general misery – a world in which, if things are left to God, life for most men, as Thomas Hobbes remarked, is 'solitary, poor, nasty, brutish, and short' – the twentieth century puts God in the dock and accuses him of talking nonsense when he claims to be loving. The idea of a loving God is so plainly irreconcilable with the fact of a suffering world that one or other has to go; and since we know that the world exists and suffers, we conclude that God does not do so. He is dead, as Nietzsche informed us, or never existed at all, as I believed for years. This is a conclusion which seems inescapable, even when we admit that most human suffering is self-inflicted or

inflicted by human beings on each other; but the problem becomes more complicated when you delve a little
deeper and are forced to admit that, since to be human is
to be free to make choices, however limited that freedom may be by our genetic inheritance, social conditioning and acquired compulsions and habits, then
the freedom to love people or to hate them and make
them suffer is part of our heritage as human beings.
This leaves out suffering caused by what the insurance
companies call 'acts of God', but once the word 'love' is
mentioned in conjunction with suffering yet another
aspect of the problem forces itself on the attention; for,
as I have already said briefly, there is a sense in which
love and suffering are Siamese twins, the one being
unable to exist without the other. A thousand Chinese
babies and their parents are drowned in a disastrous
flood by the river Yangtsze-kiang, and this is reported in
a brief and factual little paragraph on the back page of
The Times, where I read of their deaths with equanimity
and get on with the more interesting task of solving the
crossword puzzle; but when my child, mother, lover or
lifelong friend tells me that he or she has a month to live,
I suffer because I love. Only a world without love would
be a world without suffering. Perhaps the world of
reptiles and that of insects is devoid of both love and
suffering. I remember reading a book by a Dutch
entomologist who had made a study of a certain kind of
bee to be found in some profusion in the rough country
behind the sand dunes of Friesland near the Zuider Zee;
in order better to study their behaviour, he marked
various individual bees with spots of brilliantly coloured
paint and then watched them through binoculars as they
went about their apian business day by day. One day as
he was watching one of his bees flying back to the hive,
he was startled to see a spotted flycatcher leave its perch,

dash out after the bee and neatly peck off its entire back
half, abdomen and all: a disaster, however, which had
no apparent effect upon the insect's forward half — its
head and winged thorax — which continued to fly
homewards in an apparently serene beeline until the
bird, recovering from its surprise, darted out and gob-
bled up the remainder of the insect. It is doubtful
whether its loss was noticed, let alone mourned, by its
fellow bees in the hive, where love, as we understand it,
appears to be as absent as suffering, as we understand it,
was conspicuously absent during the mutilation and
subsequent death of the bee eaten by the flycatcher. So
the insect world may well be a world without either
suffering or love, but I doubt very much whether any
human being would choose to live in it, had he or she the
power to do so, rather than in the human world where
the fact that we love inevitably opens us to the experience of suffering; and I doubt, too, whether any god
worthy of the name of God would ever have dreamt of
creating such a terrible and depersonalizing neutrality
as a world without either love or suffering. So it seems to
me at least possible to argue that only a loving God
could have created a suffering world, and indeed that a
loving God could not have done otherwise.

This is not a complete answer by any means to the
problem of suffering, if indeed there is such a thing,
which I doubt; for apart from anything else it leaves out
of account the related problems of physical pain and of
suffering caused, not by love of someone else, but by
self-love. I have nothing very useful to say about physical pain, except possibly to remark upon the fairly obvious fact that it is the complement of physical pleasure,
rather as suffering is the twin of love; for the same
nerves which provide us with much of our sensual

delight in life also warn us usefully, if painfully, of those things which we should avoid as destroyers. Thus, while it is enjoyable to warm our bottoms in front of the fire, it is painful and destructive to sit on it; similarly everyone enjoys being caressed, but few much care for being hit with a sledge-hammer. However, as far as suffering caused by self-love is concerned, once again the myth of the Fall in Genesis has some cogent things to say; for if our ancestors ceased to be simian and became human at that formative mythological 'moment' when they attained self-consciousness with its accompanying psychological act of self-enthronement, presumably the kind of gnawing fear of self-dethronement and corrosive anxiety about self-ending, which everyone experiences, were born at the same time, bringing in their train the self-centred struggle to survive both personally and corporately, which everyone also knows so intimately and drearily well, and which causes so much suffering when thwarted. The lust to succeed, to beat the next person, to dominate and shine were born in Eden: lust for power, lust for success, lust for fame and its counterfeit immortality all had their origin in that God-created but snake-infested paradise, though they came into their own only when the eponymous ancestors of the human race were thrown out of it into the desert of their own creating. There they gave birth to Tillich's triarchy of human anxieties, and there poor Adam and Eve were given time before they died to sit down and try to understand what those aboriginal lusts of theirs, received as birthday presents from the snake, had done to them and their world; though I doubt whether they ever managed to understand them as well as Shakespeare did half-a-creation later:

The expense of spirit in a waste of shame
Is lust in action; and till action, lust
Is perjur'd, murderous, bloody, full of blame,
Savage, extreme, rude, cruel, not to trust;
Enjoy'd no sooner, but despisèd straight;
Past reason hunted; and no sooner had,
Past reason hated, as a swallow'd bait,
On purpose laid to make the taker mad:
Mad in pursuit, and in possession so;
Had, having, and in quest to have, extreme;
A bliss in proof, and prov'd, a very woe;
Before, a joy propos'd; behind, a dream.
All this the world well knows; yet none knows well
To shun the heaven that leads men to this hell.

Indeed, none does: at least, not in practice, though in theory the way of avoidance is clear enough; for if the self-regarding lusts which lead people into Shakespeare's hell were born at the same moment as that in which human beings enthroned themselves as God, omniscient and self-sufficient, the remedy for the suffering which comes with them and the end of the nightmare is self-abandonment and the re-enthronement of God.

That sounds simple enough, but it is much easier said than done. The old Adam, self-enthroned and self-regarding, does not die at a stroke, as St Paul discovered when he told the Christians in Rome, 'I do not understand my own actions . . . I can will what is right, but I cannot do it. For I do not do the good I want, but the evil I do not want is what I do'; and for once his meaning is made clearer in a modern translation than it is in the King James Bible without any great linguistic loss. The will is a puny thing with which to take on Shakespeare's 'perjur'd, murderous, bloody' inner compulsions to make something of ourselves by ourselves, and seldom wins; indeed, that may be inevitable, for when people imagine that they have won the battle by their own willpower, they are liable to become so arrogant and blinded by pride that they do not realize how deeply they have fallen into the trap of feeling immense self-satisfaction at the conquest of their self-centredness – 'God, I thank thee that I am not as other men are . . .' – and the last state of such people is worse than the first. The will is so much a part of the armoury of our self-assertion that usually it has to die before the true self can begin to blossom. (In strict parenthesis, if anyone does not believe in original sin, I invite him or her to watch some children at play in a primary school playground during morning break; if the spectator would prefer to attribute what he or she sees to a congenital tendency to aggressive self-assertion instead of to original sin, my only objection would be to point out that two words are preferable to seven.) But the death of the will is less likely to be an isolated psychological event than to be part and parcel of a greater process of personal bankruptcy, which is why, presumably, it was the poor in spirit, those who mourn, the meek, the weak, and those who, through inability to trust in themselves, were forced to turn elsewhere for hope and satisfaction, who were said to be blessed by Christ. It is yet another paradox, but it is one that many people have experienced, that the death of the old, striving, anxious, self-regarding and self-reliant self in some sorrow or disaster frees the true human self from servitude to Tillich's demonic trinity and from much else besides to become what it is and to grow into what it should be.

Yet that is not the end of paradox, for the new freedom to be what one should be does not bring with it an end to suffering; for since escape from suffering would involve escape from loving, there is no way in which a

God-given freedom to be truly human can possibly confer such an escape; for it is a freedom which has its origin in the discovery that one is loved by God, and its consequence is the discovery of how lovable other suffering people can be when no longer viewed as potential victims to be sacrificed on the altar of Tillich's demons of one-upmanship. If Christ was not only the window on to the true nature of God but also a revelation of what it is like to be truly human, plainly we cannot expect to escape anything – loneliness, misunderstanding, rejection, defeat, derision, or death itself – for he escaped none of those things. Escape from suffering may be included in the list of things advertised for sale by certain religious bucket shops, but it is not to be found in any catalogue of the true gifts of God; on the contrary, 'In the world ye shall have tribulation', Jesus promised his disciples according to St John, thus giving the lie to those who would have us believe that God can be relied upon at all times to pull our personal, economic and political chestnuts out of the fires of our own making, while leaving non-Christians to suffer the consequences of their own actions and indeed of the actions of others. John Betjeman's war-time poem, 'In Westminster Abbey', satirized this lie.

> Gracious Lord, oh bomb the Germans.
>   Spare their women for Thy sake,
> And if that is not too easy
>   We will pardon Thy Mistake.
> But, gracious Lord, whate'er shall be,
>   Don't let anyone bomb me.

But if tribulation in this world is the inescapable human condition, '. . . be of good cheer, for I have overcome the world', the Johannine Christ assured his disciples.

Peace beyond suffering – the other side of it – and hope beyond the nadir of despair are the true gifts of God. Those whom we love will still die, and so shall we ourselves; there is no escape from those facts of existence; but if God created life out of the wreckage of Calvary with its blood and reek of triumphant violence, he can create hope and trust out of our fear, faithlessness and despair: hope that neither the crematorium chimney nor the neat and impersonal municipal grave shall have the last word.

But renewal follows death, never precedes it; or to put this another way, the vision has to be lost in Gethsemane, or so it seems, and in the subsequent darkness at noon before the sun can rise at Easter or the Spirit descend at Whitsun: all of which is a rather pious ecclesiastical way of saying that there are times when scepticism, doubt and darkness are the order of the day, and when everything I have just said sounds like propositional nonsense. In other words, there are times when I doubt whether I believe any of it, and find myself hopelessly stuck in Gethsemane. So what do I do then?

XI

The Valley of Baca

The answer to the question at the end of the previous chapter is that, like most people, when the vision fades, I turn on the television set, do the crossword, have a drink, read a book, think of something else or immerse myself in work; and all these ways of coping with my predicament work fairly well for a time with the possible exception of self-immersion in a flurry of narcotic activism. Of course, this, too, works splendidly as an opiate for a certain length of time but, like other drugs, if long continued it can become a habit and a substitute for both vision and faith; and then the work produced becomes more and more sterile. St Paul with his usual irritating habit of being right knew all about the dangers inherent in a frantic attempt to prove something to God by trying to make good works do duty for faith; for such a course of action is essentially self-justificatory and eventually tends to turn those who indulge in it into that least attractive of human types, the do-gooder. In my less charitable moments I sometimes wonder whether the activism of today's Church, committed to everything except quietness, may not be a symptom of a hidden lack of certainty, unacknowledged and deeply buried under a feverish programme of evangelical missions and campaigns and ready-wrapped in brassy certitude: a programme which does duty for faith, but which is very different from that advocated by Isaiah, who told his contemporaries that 'in returning and rest shall ye be saved; in quietness and in confidence shall be your strength'.

Be that as it may, I doubt whether activism has ever proved to be a satisfactory way of filling the gap left when God appears to go missing for a time, which he does much more often than we care to admit; indeed, periods of time when he goes absent without leave from us are probably the norm and always have been so historically. 'Behold I go forward,' Job told his pious comforters with embarrassing honesty, 'but he is not there; and backward but I cannot perceive him; on the left hand, but I cannot behold him; he hideth himself on the right hand, but I cannot see him.' Similarly, the great deutero-Isaiah of the captivity in Babylon remarked upon the divine reticence. 'Verily thou art a God that hidest thyself,' he said; while in the first book of Samuel it is recorded of that prophet's time, the period round about 1100 BC, that 'the word of the Lord was rare in those days; there was no frequent vision'. These are isolated instances, but references in biblical history to 'the wilderness' and in subsequent religious experience to 'the dark night of the soul' are legion, and in both cases they are terms symbolic of the withdrawal or the apparent absence of God: the wilderness, a place of temptation, where men get lost and go astray like sheep and God seems to have deserted them; the dark night of the soul, a state of mind, black with mourning for the loss of God and bereft of all hope. But passage through the wilderness has not been the monopoly of the Jobs, the Isaiahs and the Samuels of this world any more than the soul's dark night has been the lodging place only of St John of the Cross and his like; artists, poets and musicians, Milton in his blindness, Beethoven in his deafness, Van Gogh in his dereliction and a host of others have known all about the wilderness and the darkness of its nights. Indeed, I sometimes think that they have explored its depths with greater courage and honesty than most other people, give or take a few contemplative saints. It was a poet, after all, who plumbed the depth of the paradox that, even though the wilderness is the *locus classicus* of no-vision, again and again it has also proved to be the birthplace of vision: 'Blessed is the man ... who going through the vale of misery use it for a well, and the pools are filled with water,' he cried, while another realized that, though the wilderness may be God-forsaken, one of God's paradoxical habits is that 'He maketh the wilderness a standing water, and water-springs of a dry ground.'

Knowing this, monks and hermits of all religions have flocked to the world's wildernesses in the hope that, with time and devotion, they may learn what it means to use the vale of misery as a well, while the dry pools of their bankruptcy are filled with water. The Egyptian desert was at one time so full of men and women in search of God's water-springs in its dry ground that it was known as the desert of the saints, while others have created mini-wildernesses of their own wherever they have settled and built themselves a house in which to explore the empty places inside themselves; for, as H. A. Williams insisted, that is the true wilderness. It has sometimes been suggested that the concrete jungle of the modern city is today's symbolic equivalent of the old biblical wilderness; that we need seek no further for a readily available symbol of the vale of misery than the streets of London or New York or any other city. But it is not true, for the city is a place of noise, distraction, crowds and perpetual activity; it is a wilderness of our own making to which we resort precisely in order to fill our days and nights with noise and to ignore the dereliction and emptiness inside ourselves. There is sufficient distraction in the city to make it splendidly difficult for us to find time off from trivia to go down into the little private deserts and solitary places inside ourselves even for a weekend's camping every now and again, let alone for long enough to find our way about there; but to pay such visits is the only way to come to terms with the inner dereliction which leaves us hyper-active and as jolly as prostitutes as we put on an act to cover our nakedness – 'Look how friendly, loving and Christian I am!' – but as dead behind the eyes as Archie Rice in John Osborne's play, *The Entertainer*. Of course, mere entry into our inner wilderness – the place of dereliction within us – does not transform it *ipso facto* into an oasis of faith, for faith and vision, as I have already said, are gifts which cannot be ordered over the counter like groceries. Instead, we have to wait upon their donor, and waiting can take two forms, waiting in solitude and waiting together with others: that is to say, the way of the hermit and the way of the monk. However, in the world in which most of us live they are by no means mutually exclusive, and both are usually combined with much jolly prostitution.

Neither way is fashionable. However, waiting is less esteemed today than doing, and the only silence one is likely to encounter nowadays in church is that occasioned by the congregation being struck dumb with dismay at some new liturgical gimmick, as I witnessed recently when a number of rather earnest young women in body stockings for no apparent reason performed a 'liturgical dance' on the chancel steps in the middle of a service. But solitary waiting upon God is even less fashionable than corporate worship, which combines a measure of doing with waiting: indeed, a fundamental and unique kind of doing-with-waiting in the form of a genuine religious dance, in which our waiting upon God is acted out in a symbolic and ceremonial re-enactment of the drama of our redemption. Put like that, it all sounds slightly mad, and the corpse of my atheism begins to revolve in its rationalist grave; but the days of my atheism are long gone, and so are the days when it was fashionable to weigh symbolic rituals and ceremonials on a pair of rationalist scales and find them wanting. The universality and primitive roots of symbolic actions and dramas have been so well established by zoologists, ethologists and anthropologists in the last fifty years or so that it is hardly an exaggeration to say that a whole new dimension of animal behaviour has been discovered which throws as much light upon human actions as it does on those of other animals. For if fish defend their territory by mimed aggression against potential intruders and indulge in elaborate courtship rituals, while birds do much the same – the whooping crane in amorous mood each spring indulges in a love dance which would add lustre to any performance by the Bolshoi Ballet, while great crested grebes are no less worthy of commendation as symbolic dancers – it is not surprising that those later products of the evolutionary process, the mammals including humans, should have inherited similar habits.

In fact, our social behaviour is, I believe, regulated and governed far more thoroughly by an intricate and largely unconscious set of evolved symbolic gestures and actions than we realize. We lower our eyes and do not stare at someone we do not know, we bare our teeth in a smile as we are introduced, keep our distance from the patch of territory occupied by someone else on the platform as we wait for a train, give the girl we are courting a box of chocolates in much the same way as a male robin feeds the female he is courting with worms, challenge each other on the football field in ritual contests for dominance, and indulge in bouts of group aggression on the football terraces with even greater ferocity than our gentler evolutionary ancestors. At cocktail parties, board meetings, military parades, royal garden parties, executions, wedding nights, and on almost every other occasion of humans meeting with other humans, our behaviour is regulated by well-understood but unstated symbolic rituals and informed by significant ceremonial gestures. We realize, express, impart to others and receive from them such fundamental messages as 'I love you' or 'Danger! Keep out!' by means of symbolic actions, expressions and gestures more frequently, more forcibly, more profoundly, more immediately and more intelligibly than in any other way; they govern the course of our ordinary social relationships long before we open our mouths to speak, and so do symbolic rituals and ceremonials govern our relationship with God, as we act out our waiting upon his advent in the great sacramental rites of the Church.

For such a purpose we come together, usually but not always, in a place set apart and filled with symbolic reminders of the interaction of those incompatibles, God and the world, spirit and stuff, time and eternity, in an architectural style specifically associated with sacredness; there we act out in mime and rite both the descent of God upon those who wait, ask, knock and trust and the taking up of the singing, praying, kneeling assembly into God by way of praise, music and incense, while at the heart of the action we eat and drink the God and go out into the world as God-bearers. That all this brings about in reality of spirit that which is mimed in symbol and gesture has to be said, for it is both true and the common experience of generations of men and women, though they may seldom be consciously aware of it; but I realize well how nonsensical it all sounds, for I used to think it so. Indeed, I still do from time to time, though happily not very often and decreasingly. It is strange, certainly, but it is no more strange than the commonly experienced miracle of a loving union of spirit brought about by a basic act of copulation repeated regularly, or, more prosaically but no less really or commonly, the friendship cemented by the symbolic sharing of a meal and a drink; 'Cheers!', 'Lovely to see you! Do have a little more.' 'Such a super evening ... You must come to us next time.' Shared actions and symbolic social rites bring about something: they are not vacuous. Konrad Lorenz in his book *On Aggression* (1966) had this to say of them:

> The austere iconoclast regards the pomp of the ritual as an unessential superficiality which diverts the mind from a deeper absorption in the spirit of the thing symbolized. I believe that he is entirely wrong ... Our fidelity to the symbol implies fidelity to everything it signifies ... The independent existence of any culture, the creation of a super-individual society which outlives the single being, in other words all that represents true humanity is based on this autonomy of the rite making it an independent motive of human action.

Moreover, if either religious experience or experience of the arts is anything to go by, there is no such thing as 'a mere symbol' any more than there is such a thing as 'a bare fact'. In religious symbols, images and rites – and in works of art – fact and significance come together into the fullness of reality as we know it, and any attempt to analyse them into their constituent parts or to divorce one part from the other both diminishes and distorts the whole, and also results in paradox.

The other form of corporate waiting on God is both more sophisticated and more monastic in the sense that it has been more highly developed by monks and nuns than by other people, though it is not practised only in monasteries; it consists of the shared office at regular intervals throughout the day and sometimes during the night too, during which there are readings, psalms are sung or recited, and prayers are said. It all sounds rather boring, pointless and dreary, and indeed it can be very dreary at times and exceedingly boring, but it is by no means always so, and it is never pointless; for even when practised only once or perhaps twice a day on a not very regular or disciplined basis, over the years it can hardly fail to have a lasting and deep effect, if only by dint of repetition. If you are forced – or perhaps choose – to say: I love America . . . or the Pope . . . or Aston Villa, often and long enough, you will almost certainly come to do so; for the images received into a person's head eventually shape and form that head for good or ill in much the same way as the content of a computer is shaped and formed when it is programmed; hence the danger of such influences as the gutter press and video nasties, and hence, too, the enormous power of advertising, political censorship and techniques of indoctrination and brain-washing. Plainly, therefore, it is important to choose with care the images which you invite into the sanctuary of your head, let alone to preserve that fundamental freedom of choice, even if your freedom to do so is strictly limited and only becomes available to you when your head has already been stocked with a mass of ready-made furniture inherited from other people. The value of the monastic offices is concentrated in the immensely rich store of images which they contain, many of them, like Jung's archetypes, of perennial power and relevance: the sea and the womb, blood and life, darkness and light, spring-time and harvest, death and rebirth, the vine and a corn of wheat. They have been forged over the ages in the crucible of the pains and prayers, fears and hopes, griefs and joys,

visions and dreams of men and women whose lives have
been invaded by God – or so they have believed – and
whose consequent understanding of themselves and the
world has been expressed in a great treasury of myth,
poetry, psalmody and symbolism; and the hope of those
who explore it from time to time is that something of the
depth of that understanding and its richness may
become their own. Personally, I have found that most of
the time the words of the prayers and the psalms and
readings fall on the dry ground of my inattention, where
they may lie forgotten in the dust for years until,
watered one day perhaps by tears of grief or joy, they
germinate and come alive; but there are other times,
too, when a familiar phrase, a passage which I have read
a hundred times or a neglected image lodges in the
forefront of my mind, and for no apparent reason puts
down roots at once, grows and blossoms. Over the
years, this process of slow germination and occasional
summer flowering has changed and enriched out of all
recognition the mental landscape in which I live. In
comparison with the more fundamental power of the
primitive sacramentalism of the great participatory
symbolic rites of the Church, it is probably true to say
that the power of the offices to influence us is limited to
the intellect, but that need hardly be held against them;
if my own is anything to judge by, the unfertilized
intellect can be a very sterile thing and in need of just
what the offices have it in their poetic, symbolic and
evocative power to bestow; though whether the
language of the reformed rites will have the same evocative power as that of the old, only time will show.

The most fundamental form of prayer, however,
underpinning all the rest, is solitary: waiting on God
alone, often in darkness and always in silence. It is
essentially a way of eschewing words and embracing

quietness, and as a result it is difficult to describe in words, though paradoxically there is a massive literature devoted to the subject, which I have no intention of trying to emulate or summarize. But there are certain things which not only can but should be said about it, and the first of them is that it is not the private preserve of the hermit, the contemplative, the mystic and the crackpot; there is a place for specialization and professionalism in almost all human activities, including this way of waiting on God, but that does not mean that only those who devote a lifetime to it may practise it. On the contrary, everyone should do so, if only because at its most basic it is an exploration of the latent possibilities, untrodden areas and unplumbed depths of the human mind, and it would be both impoverishing and a pity to die without learning something of their nature and function, let alone of their existence. It is a kind of mental pot-holing, during the course of which an attempt is made to descend as deeply as possible in a voyage of discovery into the darkness below the well-lit surface of the mind with its perpetual buzz of internal conversation. In order to do this, the flurry of words in the conscious mind has to be stilled or regulated, and there are ways of doing this: techniques of prayer – the Rosary and the Russian 'Jesus Prayer' are examples – which are not in themselves prayer at all but ways of clearing the mind's decks for the real action, which is about to begin. Prayer of this kind is practised by people of other religions, but the Christian charter for it is the command, 'Watch and pray . . . for ye know not when the master of the house cometh, whether at even, or at midnight, or at cockcrowing, or in the morning; lest coming suddenly he find you sleeping. And what I say unto you, I say unto all, Watch!' If that is the charter, the object of the exercise is to ensure that you are at home when the master of the house arrives, in the hope that you will then discover what St Paul was talking about when he said that 'the Spirit of God dwelleth in you' and what he meant when he told his correspondents in Rome that although 'we know not how to pray as we ought ... the Spirit himself maketh intercession for us with groanings which cannot be uttered'. This kind of prayer, even more than any other kind, has little or nothing to do with human striving to ascend to God, but is entirely to do with the descent of God upon those who wait and watch; the initiative is God's, the experience of his coming ours. But if you say, 'Describe it!', it is extraordinarily difficult to do so; the traditional ways of speaking of it as the experience of 'interior illumination' or the 'vision of the divine' resulting in 'ineffable joy' mean very little. All that can be said of it – and probably it will not help very much – is that it is the experience of the image coming together with that which it images, of the taking-up of the microcosm by the macrocosm, when 'One deep calleth another, because of the noise of the water-pipes: all thy waves and storms are gone over me.'

> The earthquake in the soul
> Splits the security of explanation.
> My other self, my self, my other,
> And love between, the correspondent fire;
> The image made beyond outside the self,
> The print of otherness
> With unexpected action of its own
> And all initiative:
> So rapt the feeling, some will feel it so,
> I come like passionate lover to the soul
> And rape the mystic on his bed of pain.

John Bowker

Somewhere near the place which T. S. Eliot called 'the still point of the turning world', which is in everyone, the evidence for such things happening is overwhelming, though most of us will probably never experience them so intensely or so unmistakably as described in that poem by John Bowker, from whose theological works I have already quoted. However, I suspect that this is our fault; we dare not let go, try again, trust the little rustling of the leaves as the wind of God passes by. The moments of illumination come and go, the sudden encounters with something other than ourselves take us by surprise, prayer blossoms like a flower in the darkness and fades as quickly as it opened, and like the sensible creatures we are, we pull ourselves together and cling on to a little healthy scepticism like drowning people holding to a lifeline; we do not like to boast, are too modest to believe that anything like that could happen to us, are afraid of the otherness and of going dotty – or just of being thought a bit dotty – so we let the moment slip, write off Uccello as stiff and quaint, Cézanne's *petite sensation* in the face of the natural world as the product of the artistic temperament, Otto Loewi's dream as 'probably psychological' (whatever that may mean), and Teresa of Avila as an hysteric, which she probably was, and therefore as someone whom a well-brought-up God would not dream of meeting socially. So we leave this kind of prayer to monks and nuns and lunatics, and the depths of our humanity remain unexplored, until one day, battered by despair or grief, we are driven down into the darkness inside ourselves and arrive there as strangers; frightened and ill at ease like aliens in a strange country, we do not know our way about and cannot speak the language. Yet here all our fresh springs rise into the mountain of God, and if only we knew where they were and how to drink of them, we could return refreshed and renewed to the corporate worship of the Church, let alone to the bus queues, the arguments, the death of old Aunt Mildred, and the life of that depressingly familiar and irremovable lodger in my skin – myself.

People who try to practise this kind of solitary prayer are sometimes accused of escapism and selfishness; Christianity, they are told, is about loving your neighbour, not withdrawing from him or her into introspective isolation and useless self-hypnotic exercises which cannot possibly profit anyone. Yet I believe this judgement to be completely mistaken, for love that does not put its roots down into the love of God is not what the world is dying for, and if it is important for us as individuals to learn to watch and pray and in the watching to learn something of that love, it may actually be still more important for us as a species to relearn something about our relatedness to God at depth; and if individuals do not show the way, how can anyone else follow? William Barrett, the American philosopher, from whose works I have already quoted, has made the same point; speaking of the fate of Dionysus Zagreus, who was torn to pieces by the Titans in an ancient Cretan myth, he has said this:

He who would descend into the lower regions runs the risk of succumbing to what the primitives call 'the perils of the soul' – the unknown Titans that lie within, below the surface of ourselves. To ascend again from the darkness of Avernus is, as the Latin poet tells us, the difficult thing, and he who would make the descent had better secure his lines of communication with the surface. Communication means community, and the adventurer into the depths would do well to have roots in a human community . . . He who descends must keep in touch with the surface, but on the other hand modern man may also be torn apart by the titanic forces within himself if he does *not* attempt the descent into Avernus. It is no mere matter of psychological curiosity but a question of life and death for man in our time to place himself again in contact with the archaic life of his unconscious. Without such contact he may become the Titan who slays himself. Man, this most dangerous of animals, as Nietzsche called him, now holds in his hands the power to blow himself and his planet to bits. .

To ignore that warning would be foolish. If anyone does not know how to heed it, let him take a guide; Dante took Virgil, many today follow Jung, and some travel East to find a guru; but the sovereign guide is Christ, and if the world wants to survive into the twenty-first century, it could do much worse than listen to the command he gave to his sleeping disciples when he himself prepared for his last battle and descent into hell. 'Could ye not watch with me one hour?' he said to them as they dozed the world's crisis away in a half-life of faithlessness and fear. 'Watch and pray.'

XII

Conclusion

In trying to describe the development of ideas in my head — the exploration of my own humanity — I have probably laid too much emphasis upon moments when the ordinary world has seemed to me to be transformed, moments of subjective illumination and heightened awareness, and too little upon those longer and much commoner periods when the objective world has remained very ordinary indeed, and I have plodded along with little or no vision of anything beyond its everyday ordinariness; but I have done so purposely in order to redress what seems to me to be an imbalance created by the Church, which invariably plays down the former and extols the virtues of dull perseverance and unilluminated fidelity instead. 'You will not feel anything,' the parish priest tells those about to be confirmed by the bishop; and when, not surprisingly, they *don't* feel anything, he wonders why they give up so soon and conclude that religion is not for them. I know that Uccello's *Rout of San Romano* was a great work long before it halted me in my tracks and revealed itself to me, and that it will remain just as great even if I get bored with it or pass it one day in a dyspeptic mood and see nothing much in it once again; but I am glad that none of my teachers at the Royal Academy School of Art ever said to me, 'It doesn't matter what you *feel* about works of art; all you have to do is to believe me when I tell you that they are splendid, even if they don't look it.' God is real whether I acknowledge his reality or not, but I shall only know him to be real when he becomes real

for me, and by playing down the little glimpses of God
and moments of vision in people's lives, far commoner I
believe than is usually assumed, the Church in its scepticism and fear of subjectivity can all too easily nip a
person's faith in the bud. So, while I know that perseverance in periods of darkness is a virtue to be culti-
vated and prized, I make no apology for emphasizing
the importance of those breaks in the clouds when the
sun comes out and something never seen before discloses
itself to the person with eyes to see, whether he or she be
a scientist, an artist, a child in the snow, or someone in
search of his or her own meaning and significance.

But I do apologize if, in describing my journey from
atheism to Christian belief, I have made it sound
straightforward. It has not been so. Instead, belief and
doubt, faith and scepticism, worship and boredom,
prayer and self-reliance, silence and distraction, listening and deafness, hope and dull depression, symbol and
what we mistakenly call bare fact have battled for dominance over me, while I have kept moving erratically
along a far from straight or narrow path: two paces
backwards, one sideways, with half a pace forwards
occasionally; and yet the ambiguity of these contradic-
tory signposts lining my route has at least ensured that I
should not for long treat any of them as ends in themselves, not even love or prayer, faith or worship, symbol
or silence. They are not; they are means to an end, and
that end is God – the *mysterium tremendum et fascinans* of
the eternal spirit – ultimate reality. 'Thou hast created
us for thyself,' said St Augustine in a celebrated statement (*Confessions*, Book I, ch. 1), 'and my heart shall
find no rest until it rests in thee.' Yes, indeed, but when
can anyone claim to have reached such a resting place,
or cry, 'I have arrived!'? Although Eliot began his poem
East Coker with the words, 'In my beginning is my end',

before he had finished it he turned them upside down in recognition of the endlessness of the human journey:

> Old men ought to be explorers
> Here and there does not matter
> We must be still and still moving
> Into another intensity
> For a further union, a deeper communion
> Through the dark cold and empty desolation,
> The wave cry, the wind cry, the vast waters
> Of the petrel and the porpoise.
> In my end is my beginning.

In every end there should be a beginning, in every death a resurrection, change being the quality of life and immobility that of death; but even though I know that my journey is not ended, I also know that somehow I have been brought quite a long way from the point on the road where my atheism finally collapsed and I began to thumb a lift from whatever driver of a passing ideological bus would pick me up and tell me who I was and where I was going. One of the most exciting events along the way was the discovery that science, art and Christian faith are united at their most creative depths by a common dependence upon moments of disclosure, a common belief in order, harmony and beauty, and a common recognition of the significance and value of ordinary things. This was a discovery which transformed the world into which I had been born, making sense by turning what that world used to call sense upside down, and reversing its judgements: indeed, it could hardly have done otherwise, for implicit in it was the discovery that a man whom the world had judged and hanged on a tree outside Jerusalem was the world's judge, that the poor in spirit were richer than the fat, that those who die in the world's Buchenwalds and

Dachaus are more powerful than those who put them there, and that the blind are more likely to see things worth seeing than those who pride themselves on their panoramic vision. It was a surprising discovery and not easy to get used to, though I should have been better prepared than most people for its reversals; for the artists have been overturning the world's judgements all down history, challenging people to see Rembrandt's lumpish naked women as more beautiful than Boucher's dimpled rosy pin-ups, Velazquez's derided dwarfs to be the soul of dignity, and Cézanne's monumental apples to be as noble as the Parthenon, and I had understood the artists for many years before God turned my life upside down. Meanwhile, the scientists, too, had taught me to live in a very different world from that in which I had been spawned and raised: a world in which uncertainty had replaced certitude, the growth of a mould on jelly had produced a revolution in medicine, the stone Dr Johnson kicked had turned out to be a near-empty package of electrons and protons, and the world itself a patch of mist to a passing army of neutrinos; and all this, apparently, inherent in a self-disclosing reality external to scientists, artists, the poor in spirit, and those who wait and watch.

Somehow, too, I have been given an answer to the problem of my own identity, nature and significance, which was what I was seeking when I set out in the first place. It was not the only answer available along the route, but it made sense of my experience, my humanity and the perpetually surprising loveliness of even the most unlovely of people which tends to break through the unpropitious surface from time to time when it is least expected; for if the answer to the question: What is man? is implicit in the claim that Christ was both an ordinary man of flesh and blood, and also an embodiment of a mystery which transcended his ordinariness, then the duality of my own ordinary humanity in all its uneasy marriage of body and mind, flesh and spirit, brute lump and transcendent mystery begins to be understandable, as does that of all people. He is the supreme clue both to the un-ordinariness of ordinary people, their eternal significance and value, and also to their destiny in the providence of God. Thus, I can say at last to my small cloud of unquiet corpses, *Requiescant in pace*, in gratitude to them for not allowing me to take my life for granted without asking questions about its meaning. As for myself, what is left of me, old, bald and a bit corrupt, I shall try to remember in whatever time remains to me that being is a matter of becoming, and becoming is a matter of receiving: 'He came unto his own, and his own received him not. But as many as received him, to them gave he power to become the sons of God.' I shall try to remember, too, that the becoming and the receiving depend to a greater extent than we often realize upon the images which we invite, allow and welcome into our heads, where those of this world's demons, attractive as they are, fight with the images of God for mastery over us and dictate our behaviour. 'By their fruits shall ye know them.' But since this book is about belief and not behaviour, that is another story.

Sources

p. 118   '. . . if Christ hath not . . .' 1 CORINTHIANS 15:14

p. 124   'When the doors . . .' JOHN 20:19
         'their eyes were opened . . .' LUKE 24:13–35
         '. . . none of the disciples . . .' JOHN 21:1–12
         '. . . if any man is in Christ . . .' 2 CORINTHIANS 5:17

p. 127   '. . . no man can say . . .' 1 CORINTHIANS 12:3

p. 129   'I know that thou canst . . .' JOB 42:2–6

p. 156   'I do not understand . . .' ROMANS 7:19

p. 158   'In the world . . .' JOHN 16:33
         '. . . be of good cheer . . .' JOHN 16:33

p. 160   '. . . in returning and rest . . .' ISAIAH 30:15

p. 161   'Behold I go forward . . .' JOB 23:8
         'Verily thou art a God . . .' ISAIAH 45:15
         '. . . the word of the Lord . . .' 1 SAMUEL 3:1

p. 162   'Blessed is the man . . .' PSALM 84:5–6
         'He maketh the wilderness . . .' PSALM 107:35

p. 169   'Watch and pray . . .' MARK 13:35–37

p. 170   '. . . we know not how . . .' ROMANS 8:26
         'One deep calleth another . . .' PSALM 42:7

p. 173   'Could ye not watch . . .' MARK 14:37

General

Barrett, William C., *Irrational Man*. Westport, CT, USA,
    Greenwood Press, 1977.
Bettelheim, Bruno, *The Informed Heart*. London, Thames &
    Hudson, 1960.
Bowker, John, *The Religious Imagination and the Sense of
    God*. Oxford University Press, 1978.
Frankl, Viktor, *Psychotherapy and Existentialism*. London,
    Souvenir Press, 1970.
Hardy, Alister, *The Spiritual Nature of Man*. Oxford Univer-
    sity Press, 1979.

Koestler, Arthur, *Janus*. London, Hutchinson, 1978.

Kuhn, T. S., *The Structure of Scientific Revolutions*. University of Chicago Press, 1962 (rev. edn 1970).

Lorenz, Konrad, *On Aggression*. London, Methuen, 1966.

Passmore, John, *The Perfectibility of Man*. London, Duckworth, 1972.

Read, Herbert, *Art and Society*. London, Heinemann, 1937.

Sagan, Carl, *The Dragons of Eden: Speculations on the Evolution of Human Intelligence*. London, Hodder & Stoughton, 1978.

Webb, C. C. J., *Religious Experience*. Oxford University Press, 1945.

Fount Paperbacks

Fount is one of the leading paperback publishers of religious books and below are some of its recent titles.

- [ ] THE WAY OF ST FRANCIS Murray Bodo £2.50
- [ ] GATEWAY TO HOPE Maria Boulding £1.95
- [ ] LET PEACE DISTURB YOU Michael Buckley £1.95
- [ ] DEAR GOD, MOST OF THE TIME YOU'RE QUITE NICE Maggie Durran £1.95
- [ ] CHRISTIAN ENGLAND VOL 3 David L Edwards £4.95
- [ ] A DAZZLING DARKNESS Patrick Grant £3.95
- [ ] PRAYER AND THE PURSUIT OF HAPPINESS Richard Harries £1.95
- [ ] THE WAY OF THE CROSS Richard Holloway £1.95
- [ ] THE WOUNDED STAG William Johnston £2.50
- [ ] YES, LORD I BELIEVE Edmund Jones £1.75
- [ ] THE WORDS OF MARTIN LUTHER KING Coretta Scott King (Ed) £1.75
- [ ] BOXEN C S Lewis £4.95
- [ ] THE CASE AGAINST GOD Gerald Priestland £2.75
- [ ] A MARTYR FOR THE TRUTH Grazyna Sikorska £1.95
- [ ] PRAYERS IN LARGE PRINT Rita Snowden £2.50
- [ ] AN IMPOSSIBLE GOD Frank Topping £1.95
- [ ] WATER INTO WINE Stephen Verney £2.50

All Fount paperbacks are available at your bookshop or newsagent, or they can be ordered by post from Fount Paperbacks, Cash Sales Department, G.P.O. Box 29, Douglas, Isle of Man, British Isles. Please send purchase price, plus 15p per book, maximum postage £3. Customers outside the U.K. send purchase price, plus 15p per book. Cheque, postal or money order. No currency.

NAME (Block letters) _____

ADDRESS _____

_____